AF478474

KNOW YOUR NUMBER

by Charles Misegades

DeVorse & Company, Publisher
P.O. Box 550
Marina del Rey, California 90291

KNOW YOUR NUMBER

Copyright©
by Charles Misegades

FIRST PAPERBACK EDITION 1980

ISBN: 0-87516-388-2

Printed in the United States of America
by Book Graphics, Inc., Marina del Rey, California

KNOW YOUR NUMBER

CHAPTERS

Appendix

Astrological Planetary Hours for latitudes North and South, 25 degrees through 55 degrees, January through December, shown in their Numerical Planetary Values.

Preface

This book affords the reader a completely logical, self-evident explanation of some of the deepest mysteries encountered by humanity.

Through the use of its English language cabala and astrological numerical symbols, our everyday life can be made more interesting and fulfilling.

Current events take on new meaning, great truths are laid out in easily readable words, accidents and mysteries are easily explained.

This work is based on a numerical system, so simple in its application, that all life becomes an open book. The two phrases around which this book is written; — Man know thyself, and, As above, so below, create a perfect testimonial for the Tropical Zodiac and Astrology.

Our cosmic clock matches perfectly our every-day time piece, as well as our own bodies. All words can be translated to simple numbers from one through nine, and, counted, not on computers, but on our own two hands.

One cannot read this book and not benefit from it.

Most astrologers agree that we earthlings are on the cusp of the Aquarian age. Thus the intuitive faculty becomes the next most necessary development for this new period. This book, through its English language cabala, affords the reader an ingenious method for developing this mental extension.

Numbers are the key to this astrological interpretation.

Chapter 1
Fringe Knowledge

Numbers, numbers, numbers, — we seem to be swamped by them. Addresses, zip codes, telephone, social security, clothing sizes, prices, licenses, accounts, catalog, time, distance and etc. In this age of mechanization we have expanded our use of numbers to such an extent that we tend to think in terms of numbers. We still have our alphabet and words which we use in speech and writing. In fact, our vocabularies and publications have expanded almost as much as our numbers and computers.

Psychologically this may be one of the main causes for our runaway inflation.

Algebra, calculus and geometry are advanced forms of mathematics used by scientists and engineers in solving complicated equations. But all this is done through the use of simple numbers, one through nine, and letters of the alphabet, from A to Z. The most complicated equation in the universe is you and me!

We have read much about mental power, our divine potential and that basically we are all number (1). But that is just an abstract beginning. In the next state of our awareness we find that no (2) are alike. How does all this come about? Is this just a lot of double talk? Not on your life! Because that is where it all starts, with your life! Your birthday!

Your birthday when added to a single digit is your number, — your life. So is the total date on which you were born. These are fateful numbers that we cannot change. This is your starting point in this life and you can take it from there. This book will tell you where and how in chapters (3), (5) and (9). In chapter (6) you can re-learn your alphabet. In chapter (6) of this book is an original English language cabala, explained, tried, tested and proved in the remaining chapters of this writing.

In our Holy Bible of the Christian world, we are told that we are created in the image of deity, and, as such, we are divine creatures. In our constitution we are told that we are a free people, with freedom of choice and speech. All this is acknowledged as true, yet, when we look around us at the many problems in our local, state and national environment, one is led to the belief that somewhere along the path we must have surrendered our divine rights. Therefore, it is the purpose of this book to try to put first things first and establish some order to the thought process and avail to one and all a reasonable chance to create order out of chaos.

It has been said that; God geometrizes. As one looks to the heavens, quantities and distances boggle the mind. Ad-Infinitum, becomes a living reality.

Our educational institutions treat mathematics as a requirement in the academic field, but only so far as a means to communicate cost, quantity, distances and identities in our arts, business and scientific fields. To step mentally beyond this academically accepted field, or, scope of numbers, leads one to the fringe area of accepted knowledge. It is in this fringe area of our knowledge that numbers can become more than just numbers. In fact, they can become a language in themselves.

In the early days of Greece, Plato suggested to his contemporaries that they should know themselves. Man know thyself, was the unliberated saying passed down to the succeeding generations. The inference was that humans, being conscious living entities, are a microcosmic reflection of the macrocosmic heavens, ad-infinitum, in which we move and have our being.

In recent years knowledge about humans and their universe has increased tremendously, mostly through research and development in various academic fields. For instance, four hundred million degrees centigrade is quite a figure of heat. This is eighty thousand times the Sun's surface temperature, which is estimated at five thousand degrees centigrade. The scientists are able to do this through the use of magnetic bottles.

In Pasteur's time, his research proved that the earth's

magnetic field was a very potent factor in the ripening process. Since his day, research has shown that this magnetic force occurs in all of nature, in all organic compounds. Magnetism also causes seeds to germinate at many times their normal speed. Experiments with green tomatoes, placed inside a magnetic field, showed that they ripen four to six times faster when exposed to the south pole of a bar magnet, or, open end of a horseshoe magnet. Seeds and tomatoes are organic compounds with enzyme systems. So are human bodies.

Living things respond to musical vibrations as well. Harmonious music soothes, and, discordant music irritates. Much research has been done with music, as well as color. One Japanese experimenter even placed earphones on a tomato and played soothing music to it, and, ended up with a four and one half pound tomato!

Our sun is a gigantic electro-magnet, and, so are all the stars. Planets also are known to generate magnetic fields much like that of our earth. The human brain has a positive and negative magnetic polarization. The center of the forehead is negative and the base of the brain at the back of the head is positive. Our brains have the characteristics of radio senders and receivers. The mental signals sent out and received by individuals have the peculiar ability to be translated into emotional moods, attitudes and symbols.

Research done by the American Institute of Medical Climatology in Philadelphia in 1961, confirmed that police, fire, hospital and industrial records showed peaks and troughs corresponding to the times of the new and full moon periods. Other studies indicate that the biological rhythms of all life forms, plant, animal and human are inseparable from barometric pressure changes, atmospheric, electricity, ion density, sun spot cycles and other stellar and planetary influences.

With all our research and development to date, which has given our society so many clues to the phrase, Man Know Thyself, much of our academic and medical establishment still is reluctant to accept the evidence into practice. The arrested mentalities of persons, high in office in the academic and medical fields, continue to frown on the stellar science of astrology. We are supposed to be living in a free society, yet, our leaders in the academic and astronomical fields fall into the same dilemma as the Russian Communists when they continue to refuse to accept, or, acknowledge the validity of the planetary influences in our everyday society.

The announcement that Sputnik 1 was orbiting the earth, shocked the American public out of their smug complacency. Leading scientists were called to the White House, and, after much discussion, N.A.S.A. came into being. We were then on our way to catch up with the Russians.

Out of the discussions between American scientists and congressional committees, the conclusions were not encouraging. Billions of dollars would be needed, and, even though the money was promised and things began in earnest, the Russians always seemed to be doing more. Vast numbers of people in many countries began to believe that scientific achievement flourished better under a centralized communistic system where no conservative reactionaries could retard progress. Most thought that the Russians would be the first to put a man on the moon.

Then out of the blue, Nikita S. Khrushchev implied that the Russians were not in a hurry to put a man on the Moon. On October 25th, 1963, Khrushchev's public statement confirmed his implication. Actually the Russians were telling the truth. They had a problem that their scientists couldn't solve. They had found that after a solar flare occurs, the amount of ultraviolet and other rays traveling through the solar system is sufficiently potent to fry a man in a space capsule. The Russians had found a way to predict solar flares up to a few hours in advance, long enough to get a man orbiting the earth back to his base, but, not far enough in advance to save a man on his way to the moon.

The first direct measurements of plasma fluxes in space were made by the Soviet lunar and interplanetary space stations. Plasma being the fourth state of matter, an ionized gas which differs from an ordinary gas in that it is a good conductor of electricity, and, it is affected by a magnetic field. The solar wind consists of plasma and thus is distorted by the magnetic forces around the earth, but, it gives advance hints when solar flares are occurring. The surface of the earth is protected from the rays resulting from solar flares by its atmosphere and its magnetic field. No such protection exists in space.

The Russians had discovered how dangerous space can be. They thought that the Americans were insane in the attempt to beat the U.S.S.R. at the expense of the lives of their astronauts. The Russians were content to let the United States take the lead from there, but, were baffled as to why the Americans were so reckless in the face of the solar flare problem.

Much to the embarrassment of the Russians and to the professional American astronomers, who refuse to recognize the stellar science of astrology, the N.A.S.A. officials were more open minded. A chap named Nelson proved to these men that through the study of the planets, it was possible to predict solar flares to within less than (12) hours when they would occur, and, that the predictions could be made for as many years in advance as may be required.

The success to date of the space program tends to prove the value of an open mind in the pursuit of knowledge. The reader of this work will, in turn, be required to do the same. There are many other works on astrology and numbers, but, I believe this work to be unique and original in journalistic channels.

One glaring fact that stands out above all else, as the result of our space program, is the one that reveals the physical limitations of the human body. We are definitely mental entities, inhabiting our water-sack bodies like shells. But we do have wonderful possibilities for growth, if we can keep an open mind.

Chapter 2
Beyond the Fringe

It is not the purpose of this book to explain life, death or reincarnation. It is the purpose of this work to give enough information, concrete evidence and experience, to raise the consciousness sufficiently to be able to gain a little more knowledge about ourselves, and, our relationship to our universe. At least a little more than that which is afforded in the academic field of our present institutions.

The expression, — Man Know Thyself, is the greatest clue as to the means of achieving this knowledge.

Now, there is a truth that states; Humans are born with the seed of their own destruction within them. Until we become consciously aware of the vaster side of ourselves, our mental and spiritual, we will continue to sow and reap the fruits of that seed. The basic nature of this seed is called fear, — fear of the unknown.

As far as the physical world is concerned, the first manifestation of fear of the unknown is felt in the psyche at birth and is called, — birth trauma. As a matter of fact, fear, or, something very closely related to it, is set up in the psyche of all living things when one of those things is about to make a move from a point with which it is familiar, to one which it is not.

If we can accept this as being true, then we must suppose that fear is a natural property of the psyche, from amoeba to the complex human.

To gain a little broader understanding in the academic fringe area of accepted knowledge, such as astrology and numerology with which this work deals, one subjects oneself to ridicule by the established academic frame-work of our society. Fear of ridicule will have to be faced with courage, conviction and knowledge. Just reading such material suggests a ready, willing and open mind, which, is most necessary to learn or gain from this field of knowledge.

It has been said; To know the world of matter is to know the world of non-matter, which is the world of mind. To know the world of mind is to have cosmic-consciousness. Whether we know this, or, are aware of this, or not, matters little. We are all growing, living, evolving entities destined to know eventually. For we are all moving in and with the light in the same direction, the light being our Sun and solar system.

In thinking about the subject of matter, and, realizing at the same time the vast amount of scientific data regarding the nature of matter that has been compiled by the scientists, one may tend to conclude that the scientist is in a much better position to receive cosmic-consciousness than anyone else. Of course such a conclusion would not be true, for, all who are genuinely creative, are in tune with the cosmic mind.

A thinking student in physics soon learns that there is no such condition as matter, — per se. Therefore one does not ask; What is matter?, expecting to get an answer, any more than one would ask; How high is up? Rather one comes to know by more advanced levels of thought on the subject, that matter, or, what we believe to be matter, is just a condition, which, is the result of activity.

There is an energy exchange of a very intense nature going on between the many particles of that microscopic bit of substance referred to as the atom. This exchange is known as activity, or, work. This work in turn sets and keeps the atom as a bonded unit in motion. A portion of this work in the atom produces two different types of motion, or, levels of exchange called heat and electricity.

The laws of physics state, that, a body once set in motion will continue in a straight line unless acted upon by an external force. The fact is that three-dimensional matter cannot move in a straight line, because a straight line denotes a perpetual and unbroken form of motion. Physical matter moves not only in wave motion, but, also in periodical bundles or quanta. The cause of this motion is due to the nature of the underlying fabric of space.

The space comprising the three-dimensional universe is an

electromagnetic field that is constantly returning to its center. Our entire universe is simply a big cosmic atom. However, in order to comprehend the concept of a cosmic atom, we have to begin by studying its working parts, the microscopic atoms.

Every atom has its own space in which particles move, and, this space consists of a viscous type substance that exudes from the core of the atom in a series of arc lines. These arc lines drive the electron bodies outward from the core, or, nucleus, and, draw them back again. As this alternating magnetic force expands the orbital field of the electrons, it creates a positive electrical flow, and, as it draws the electrons back to the center, it produces a positive magnetic field. This magnetic field of attraction becomes denser, and, of greater tensile strength to the inverse square of the distance of the outer electrons from the nucleus.

While the electron is described as an energy charge, it must also be considered to have specific structure. This structure, consists of four lines of energy crossing one another at the exact center of each line. In addition, each line has a series of nodes placed alternately along its axis which builds up in density as it approaches the hub, or, center of the electron. Here they join and form a relatively larger node of greater magnetic intensity. Each of these nodes emits negative electrons which are very much smaller units of energy than the positive electron, by many thousands of times. These units of energy are the result of the electron's effort to get rid of the force that was applied to it in projecting it into orbit.

The atom is truly the mystery of the universe. It contains so many properties that one could go on forever, and, never touch on all of these properties and the things that they are capable of performing. With their vital substances they paint and mold the universe. They are the very stuff that dreams are made of. The gray matter in the head, called the brain, is made up of billions of them, and, when we think our thoughts squeeze some of the (juice) out of them in the form of neuron showers. Rub certain molecules of them gently, and they give up some of their energies in static electricity. Hit some too hard, and their energies will erupt in violent winds of death and destruction.

Today most educated folks know the word, fission, means to create a cleavage in a single unit. In fissioning atoms, a stream of extremely high speed protons are fired at the atoms and eventually the force field that surrounds the proton crashes into the force field of one of the orbiting bodies of the atom with the driving impact of millions of electron volts. The reaction of this applied force is heat, light, force and the radiation of ions, or, negative electrons, erupting from deeper layers of the atom.

Now the purpose in explaining the activity of atom fissioning is to point out to the reader, who might be unfamiliar with the subject, that, notwithstanding all the above mentioned force that is brought to bear on the atom, no actual cleavage or split has occurred. To understand this, we must first realize that there is no such thing as matter <u>and</u> energy. While we have referred to the atom as being a (body), and, electrons as having (structure), we must not let these words lead us into the belief that the universe is made up of two different kinds of substance, and, that the substance called (matter) exists as ultimate bits, or, pieces. An atom is made up of a number of force fields, with each of these force fields having its own particular rate of motion, or, vibration.

Now if any of this is clear, it should become apparent to the reader that all that happens to the atom when fissioned is to greatly expand the field of operation of the outer shells in reference to the innermost ones, called the nucleus, thereby giving the atom a larger volume of space in which to work.

In thinking of the world around us, we automatically conjure up the feeling called solidness, and, then imagine it to be a property of this world, when in fact, it is but a sensory measurement of our so-called self. By use of our imagination we are able to seed our subconscious mind to use these magical thoughts to create our realities.

There are a number of so-called highly educated men and women who shy away from the use of metaphysics and occult teachings as something too nebulous and vague. These same people will be found using equally vague and abstract hypotheses in approaching a given subject. For instance, many otherwise great scientific persons will look down their long, superior noses at you if you mention the possibility of an individual surviving bodily death, much less that they can be contacted and conversed with. Yet, these same people will look at you with a straight face while trying to explain the atom. Still the only way that they have of knowing that such a particle exists, is by mathematical equations. In the realness of things, figures, or, numbers, are nothing more than symbols, and, have no more concrete basis than does anything else.

If you doubt that figures are more than mental abstracts that aid one in postulating a mental construction so that one may deal a little better with it in our three-dimensional world, just try going into the division of matter and see what happens to the so-called concrete figures. For example, take the simple problem of the postulated zero, (0). This sign stands for what we conceive as nothing. But, one cannot arrive at such a mental concept, in any state of consciousness. However, this sign is created anyway, perhaps in order to save one's sanity. More likely, though, it is used as a force against the abstract (unseen) world, to set it into motion towards the concrete (seen) world. So now the hypothetical (nothing) becomes an x-force that, in some way or manner, is used to materialize a concrete whole number called (one), or, the beginning of substance in the three-dimensional world. Of course, in postulating this whole number one must ignore an infinity of fractions extending in both directions, from (0) to (1) and from (1) to (2), and, plus or minus from the decimal.

Physical beings must resort to some compromise of mind with matter until such time as the material brain has developed into a better vehicle for the psyche to work through. For the vast uninitiated majority it is best for them to keep to the assumption of a definite beginning and end to things. For the learned, they eventually come to the conclusion, sooner or later, that there is an ultimate force which exceeds description, and, in which we move and have our being.

Chapter 3
Numbers and the Zodiac

This book deals with numbers as symbols which we merge with sounds and letters of our English alphabet. We also identify numbers with the planetary bodies in our solar system. In the process we reduce all additions to a single digit of one through nine. The reason that this is done, is to stick to the formula of wisdom conveyed to us through the phonetic vibratory forces that are built into our own bodies and our solar system. As above, so below, — becomes our guide to the whole process.

To correlate planets to the numbers and numbers to the biological correspondents, we will refer only to known, or, accepted data that can be found in other texts. This will help to reduce the research and much repetition.

Starting with our Sun as the prime energizer of our solar system, we assign numbers (1) and (4). Number (1) to represent the yearly cycle and number (4) to signify the four seasons, or, the four changes in our cycle around the Sun. Biologically, the Sun rules the heart in the human anatomy. The heartbeat in the normal human is roughly (72) to the minute. The average life span for the normal average human is roughly (72) years. Under normal conditions the average human breathes, inhales and exhales, about four complete breaths to the minute. The time motion of our earth on its axis is four minutes for each degree. Fourteen hundred and forty minutes to complete the (360) degree rotation. Note (1440) added, (1) plus (4) plus (4) plus (0) equals (9), and, (360) added, (3) plus (6) plus (0) equals (9). Number (9) is considered the human number. All numbers when added can be reduced to a single digit of (1) through (9).

The Sun in its precession of the equinoxes takes about (72) years to recede (1) degree. It takes 2,160 years (30 x 72) to move or pass through (1) sign of our zodiac, and, 25,920 years to complete the 360 degrees. Note (72), or (7) plus (2) equals (9), (2,160), or (2) plus (1) plus (6) plus (0) equals (9), and, (25,920), or (2) plus (5) plus (9) plus (2) plus (0) equals (18) or (9). The human body has (9) orifices; (2) eyes, (2) ears, (2) nostrils, (1) mouth, (1) penis, and (1) rectum.

Other astrological texts, numerous in number, can be used for further descriptions of the planetary bodies, Sun, Moon and etc. For our purposes it is sufficient to define the solar influence as individualistic, masculine, authoritative, hot, dry, prime and positive. It is usually described as a complete circle or number (1) and considered as the hour hand of our zodiacal clock. In the divine geometry, the Sun is described and symbolized by the complete circle with the dot in the center.

Next, or, second number for our consideration is that of the Moon. Here we assign two numbers also, (2) and (7). The Moon's cycle is roughly (27) days, (7) hours and (43) plus minutes. Its influence is secondary to the solar orb. It is considered as the second hand of our cosmic clock. It is negative and moist and has much magnetic affinity with all fluids in our body, in the atmosphere and the ocean tides. It is also considered domestic in its influence and has considerable influence over females, mating and growth. The menstrual periods of the female of the human species roughly corresponds to the lunar cycle of (27) days. In human births the Moon's position in the zodiac at conception usually corresponds to the rising zodiacal degree of the actual birth. This lunar body also has much influence over all bodily functions. It may be noted that the numbers assigned to this body when added, (2) plus (7) equal (9), which corresponds also to the (9) number of the human orifices of the body. The number (2) is associated with the new Moon lunation and all that it implies, and, the number (7) is associated with the full Moon. Six houses removed from the beginning of our zodiacal wheel is the cusp of the (7th) angle of Venus rulership. The Moon is exalted in the 2nd zodiacal sign of Taurus, also of Venus rulership. Six signs removed from the lunation point the Moon reaches the full light. Note; (6 x 30) degrees equals (180) degrees of (1) plus (8) plus (0) equals (9), or, the growth cycle of the Moon and the total of the Moon's numbers (2) plus (7) to (9). In the divine geometry the Moon is symbolized by the half circle or the crescent.

Number three is next in the sequence of our numbers and it is associated with Jupiter. It is considered positive and negative. It is positive in connection with the (9th) angle and negative when associated with the (12th) angle. It is also termed moist and warm, also, benefic. One plus two gives us our three. The mating of the positive and the negative denotes progressive growth and expansion, both mentally and physically. In the human body it has considerable influence over metabolism, the adrenals and the blood. It represents the trinity in all of nature. In the divine geometry it is symbolized by the perfect equilateral triangle.

Number (5) is the middle number of our system, or, our sequence, and, it is considered quite neutral. It is associated with Mercury in our solar system. It has much influence over communication and transportation. Mercury usually takes on considerable coloring from the sign and planet that is in closest configuration with it in the zodiac. It is interesting to note that this number (5) when added to the first four numbers of our group gives us our (6), (7), (8) and (9). (5) plus (1) equals (6), (5) plus (2) equals (7), (5) plus (3) equals (8) and (5) plus (4) equals (9). In the human body, Mercury is said to rule over the lungs, bowels, arms and hands. It is of additional interest to note that each hand has (5) digits.

In the divine geometry it is symbolized by the (5) pointed star. This star is created by starting with the (3rd) sign of the zodiac, Gemini, ruled by Mercury, and drawing a line through the wheel to the (8th) angle cusp, then to the (1st) angle cusp, then to the (6th) angle cusp, then to the (11th) angle cusp and then back to the (3rd) angle cusp. In this figure we have a perfect (5) pointed star drawn with (5) lines and linking both cusps ruled by Mercury, number (5). When we add the angle number values we get, (3) plus (8) plus (1) plus (6) plus (11) plus (3) to a total of (32), or (3) plus (2) equals (5). When we add the planetary rulership values of the sign cusps directing our inscribed star we get, Mercury (5) plus Mars (9) plus Mars (9)

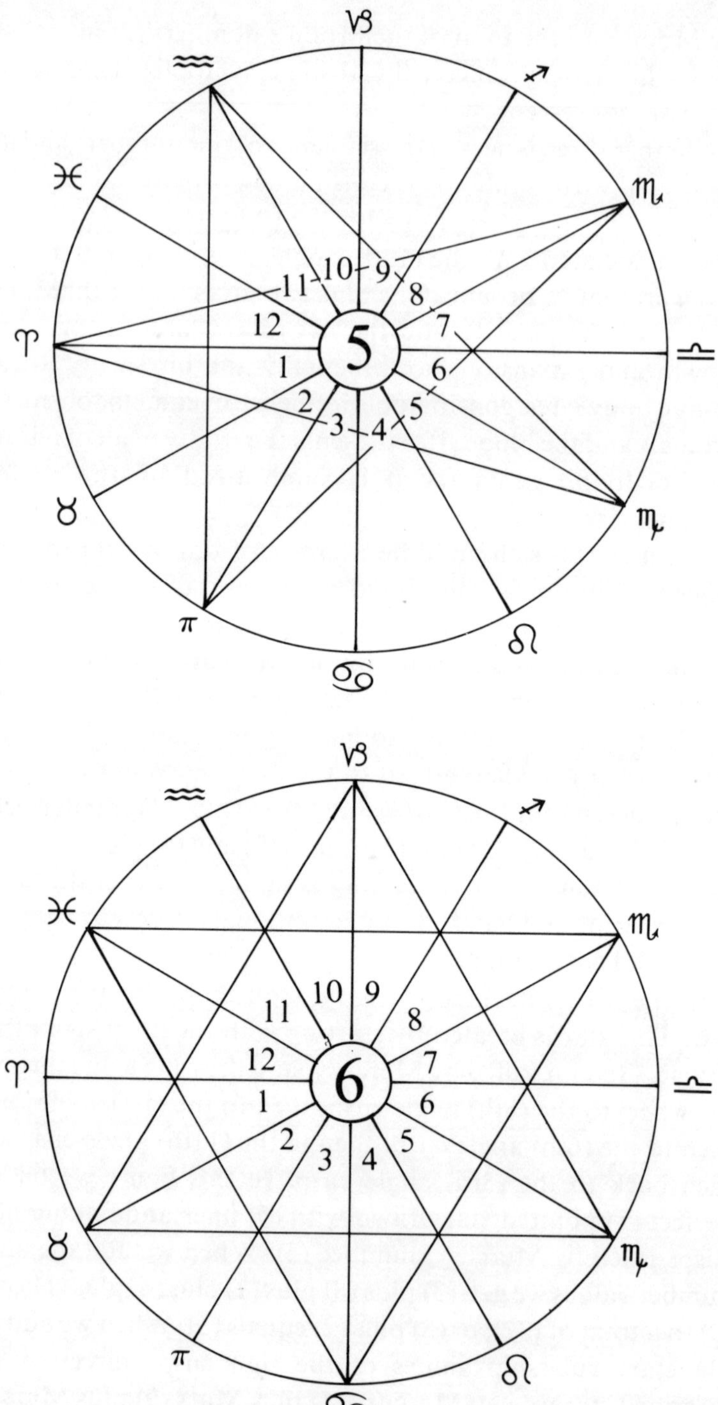

plus Mercury (5) plus Saturn (8) and Mercury (5) to a total of (41), or (4) plus (1) equals (5). Also we may note that the (5th) angle of the zodiac is ruled by the Sun, numbers (1) and (4), or (1) plus (4) equals (5).

Number (6) in our sequence is associated with Venus as its planetary significator. It is considered favorable, but, negative and feminine. This is the number of harmony and love. In the human body it has rulership over the throat and the kidneys. A triangle is a symbol of the trinity, and, in the astrological lore, 120 degrees is considered the most favorable aspect between planetary bodies and signs. It may be noted that the triangle has (3) sides to it and is associated with the planet Jupiter. In astrological books, Venus is considered as the lesser fortune and Jupiter the greater fortune. Aspects in astrological charts tend to bear this out. It is of interest to note, that, in the divine geometry, it takes (2) equilateral triangles to form the perfectly balanced (6) pointed star. To construct this figure in the astrological wheel, we commence with the second house, or, angle ruled by Venus. We have the cusp of the (2nd), (6th) and (10th) as the (3) points of the first triangle. Starting with the cusp of the (4th) angle we have the (4th), (8th) and the (12th) cusps as the (3) points of our second triangle. Thus we have a perfect (6) pointed star drawn with (6) lines. Adding the numbers of the angles involved we have (2) plus (6) plus (10) for the first triangle, and, (4) plus (8) plus (12) for our second triangle. When we add these numbers we get (42), or, (4) plus (2) equals (6). Remember that we started with the cusp of the (2nd) and the cusp of the (4th), so, when we add (2) plus the (4), we get our (6) value. The rulership of the cusps of the angles involved are Venus (6), Mercury (5), and Saturn (8) for the first triangle, and, Moon (2) — (negative value of the Moon because of the negative sign rulership), Mars (9) and Jupiter (3) for the second triangle. When we add these values, (6) plus (5) plus (8) plus (2) plus (9) plus (3) we get (33), or, (3) plus (3) equals (6).

Number (8) of our sequence is associated with Saturn in our zodiac. This planetary value is associated with limitation, karma and destiny. Number (8) is formed with two interlocking circles, similar to hand cuffs. The astrological influence under adverse Saturn directions bear this out. One actually feels shackled and restrained. Even the planet itself in the heavens depicts this symbolization, with the — (Rings of Saturn). In the human anatomy, Saturn rules the bony structure of the body, and, the knees and ankles in particular. Saturn is associated with age and cold. There is no greater limitation than age. This body is also associated with time. Our yearly cycle, days, months and years, is measured by our earth's rotation and movement around the solar orb. The (365) days and our (12) months match the zodiac of the heavens. The (3) plus (6) plus the (5) total to (14) or (1) plus (4) equals (5). The (12) (1) plus (2) equals our (3). Mercury's number (5) when added to Jupiter's number (3) gives us our (8), Saturn's value. Time on our clocks is measured by hands and numbers. Mercury (5) rules hands and communication. Jupiter (3) rules the (12th) angle of the zodiac, that of limitation symbolized by Saturn (8). Jupiter also rules the (9th) angle of the zodiac symbolized by the half horse and half man. Horse racing is greatly influenced by this planetary body. Also, at most race tracks, the (8th) race is the feature race of the day. It is usually a race requiring much stamina and ability, usually quite a test for the winner of such an event. Saturn number value (8) is often referred to as the tester.

In the Chaldean order of planetary hours, starting with the Sun, we have in positive and negative sequence, (1)-(6)-(5)-(2)-(8)-(3) and (9), or, Sun, Venus, Mercury, Moon (for the earth), Saturn, Jupiter and Mars. The first three named are the closest to the Sun, (inside the earth's orbit) and Saturn, Jupiter and Mars are the outside planets. When we use the Sun as the ruler of the heart of the zodiacal wheel, and, start from the center and proceed outwardly to the cusp of the (2nd) angle, ruled by Venus, with a projected or inscribed line and continue the sequence to the cusp of the (3rd) angle, ruled by Mercury, then to the (4th) angle, ruled by the Moon, then across through the heart of the wheel to the opposite sign, or, cusp of the (10th) angle, ruled by Saturn, then to the cusp of the (9th) angle, ruled by Jupiter, and then to the cusp of the (8th) angle, ruled by Mars, and then back to the heart of the wheel to repeat the

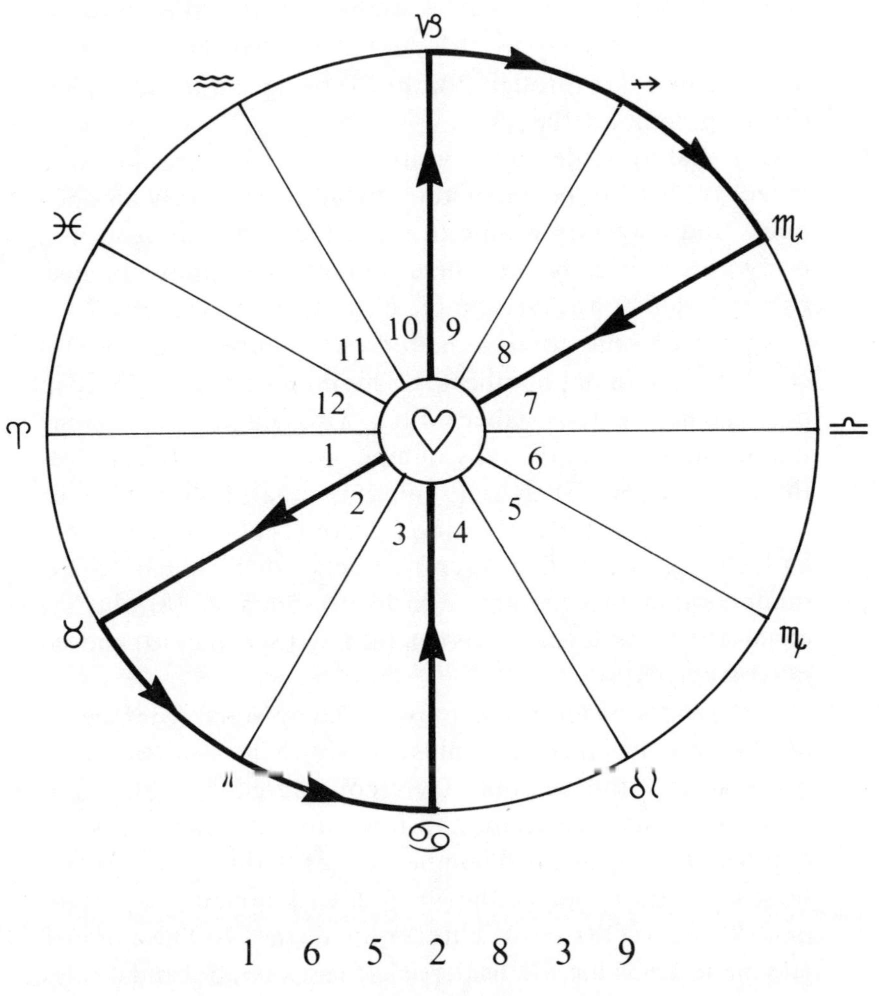

1 6 5 2 8 3 9

NUMBER (8)

cycle, or, complete the figure. This sequence forms the perfect figure (8). When the numbers of the planets (1) plus (6) plus (5) plus (2) plus (8) plus (3) plus (9) are added we get (34), or, (3) plus (4) equals (7). This seven represents the (7) visible planetary bodies of our zodiac after which all our days of the week are named. They are also symbolical of all the numbers of our system of (1) through (9), the (4) being similar to (1) and (7) being similar to the (2).

Our destiny is definitely written in the heavens and in a language that can be understood by all. Life is truly an open book, and, anybody willing to make the effort can read it in every aspect of daily life. There is much more in our English cabala, but, first we must complete our number sequence.

Next we come to the end of our number sequence in consideration of our number (9). This number is symbolized in our zodiac by the planet Mars. This number has some interesting facets in that any number added to it always gives the same number. Such as; (9) plus (1) equals (10), or (1) plus (0) equals (1), (9) plus (2) equals (11), or (1) plus (1) equals (2), and etc. Also the first four numbers when added to the numbers that precede nine add to (9). Such as; (8) plus (1) equals (9), (7) plus (2) equals (9), (6) plus (3) equals (9) and (5) plus (4) equals (9).

In the zodiacal wheel, the houses ruled by Mars, Aries the 1st and Scorpio the 8th, add (1) plus (8) to (9). Mars rules the head, genitals and the rectum. It is considered hot, dry and masculine. Passion, desire and force are attributed to Mars number (9). It is the third number of the (3), (6), (9) trio. When these numbers are added the (9) tends to dominate. (3) plus (6) plus (9) equals (18), or (1) plus (8) equals the (9). This number and planetary value is considered as the sex symbol and it rules the sex organs. This number (9) also symbolizes humanity's (9) physical orifices.

The symbol of the number (9), the circle with the adjacent, or, perpendicular line, conveys completion. The circle symbolizes the total and the line symbolizes a barrier, or end. We have noted that any number when added to this number (9) always equals that number. We can also note that all our numbers when added, (1), (2), (3), (4), (5), (6), (7), (8), (9) total to (45), or (4) plus (5) equals (9). The force in this number can be used either constructively or destructively. Mars is considered war-like and aggressive. When controlled, it is a force for good. When it is abused, it can be quite destructive. In the astrological charts the aspects tell the story. Sextile, (60) degrees adds to (6). This is Venus' number, the lesser fortune, but, considered favorable. The trine (120) degrees adds to (3). This is Jupiter's number, the greater fortune and considered very favorable. Also, the (6) and the (3) add to nine, (9). So, under these aspects we can expect favorable results from the number (9). The square aspect (90) degrees, adds to Mars number, as does the opposition of (180) degrees, (1) plus (8) plus (0) equal (9). These aspects to the number Mars (9) are considerably negative and violent. Number (9) is the number of humanity. As noted by our descriptions of the numbers (1) and (2), the sun's 72 years cycle, (7) plus (2) equals (9) and the moon's numbers (2) and (7) equal (9).

In covering our number symbols, one through nine, we have tried to show the relationships between the numbers and the planetary bodies together with the biological correspondencies. Before going on to the astrological signs of the zodiac, we might note that we do have (3) more planets that are invisible, to the naked eye when viewing the heavens. These are Uranus, Neptune and Pluto. I might mention that though we do not assign house rulership to these bodies, they do have a definite influence in the astrological relationship to our numbers. Through personal research, I have found that these planets act as higher octaves of Venus, Mercury and Mars. So, leaving them without description except to mention that Uranus is eccentric and erratic in its nature with the numerical value of (6), and, rules the thymus and pituitary glands in the physical body. Neptune is either inspirational or confusing by aspect. It is the higher octave of Mercury and its number equivalent is (5). In the physical body this planet rules the Pineal gland, which is dormant in most individuals, but, quite active in psychics and occultists. Pluto is the higher octave of Mars and is associated with number (9). It is a group influence of a karmic nature, and, has a subconscious effect on all humans. Those folks who learn to seed and control their subconscious mind tend to mitigate its effects.

In considering the numerical values of the astrological signs of the zodiac, we find that they are quite simple in as much as they reflect the same values as the rulerships on the cusp of each house. They are as follows;

Aries, ruled by Mars is a (9) value.

Taurus, ruled by Venus is a (6) value.

Gemini, ruled by Mercury is a (5) value.

Cancer, ruled by the Moon has a (2) and (7) value, (both numbers relate to this sign).

Leo, ruled by the Sun has a (1) and (4) value, (and both numbers relate to this sign).

Virgo, is ruled by Mercury and has a (5) value.

Libra, is ruled by Venus and has a (6) value.

Scorpio, is ruled by Mars and has a (9) value.

Sagittarius, is ruled by Jupiter and has a (3) value.

Capricorn, is ruled by Saturn and has an (8) value.

Aquarius, is ruled by Saturn and also has an (8) value.

Pisces, is ruled by Jupiter and also has a (3) value.

In passing we might note that the Sun and the Moon influence only one sign, but, have a double number significance. Mercury, Venus, Mars, Jupiter and Saturn have influence over (2) zodiacal angles. Uranus, Neptune and Pluto are always considered by angular position and by their aspects to the other planetary bodies. They never have reference to house rulership though they can be more potent in action in signs in which they have affinity. Any good astrological text can relate this to the readers so interested.

Consolidated Recap

	Planet	Sign		Body Rulership
1	Sun	Leo	♌	Heart-Back & Spleen
2	Moon	Cancer	♋	Stomach & Breasts
3	♃ Jupiter	Sagittarius & Pisces	♐ ♓	Adrenals-Skin-Blood Thighs & Feet
4	☉ Sun	Leo	♌	Heart-Back & Spleen
5	☿ Mercury	Gemini & Virgo	♊ ♍	Thyroid-Lungs-Arms Hands & Bowels
6	♀ Venus	Taurus & Libra	♉ ♎	Thymus-Throat- Lower Jaw & Kidneys
7	☽ Moon	Cancer	♋	Stomach & Breasts
8	♄ Saturn	Capricorn & Aquarius	♑ ♒	Bones-Knees-Calves & Ankles
9	♂ Mars	Aries & Scorpio	♈ ♏	Head-Sex Organs Bladder & Rectum
6	♅ Uranus			Pituitary Gland
5	♆ Neptune			Pineal Gland
9	♇ Pluto			Subconscious Mind

Days of the Week

Sunday (1) and (4)	Monday (2) and (7)	Tuesday (9)
Wednesday (5)	Thursday (3)	Friday (6)
Saturday (8)		

Chapter 4
Helpful Hints and Mercury Retrograde

There are in the field of medicine many factors relative to the treatment of disease that are directly influenced by the astrological signs and planets. We do not intend to try to give medical advice, but, we do want to let the reader know that the numerical date and the planetary aspects can and do affect favorably, or, adversely, the result of medical treatment. By selecting a favorable date, patients can help themselves and their doctors to facilitate successful treatment, or healing.

As any doctor knows, the force that motivates the heartbeat comes from within that organ. All healing for human ills comes from this inner source. We have shown in the previous chapter, that all physical manifestation can be traced to our hypothetical atom. The harmony that we can establish in our lives, bodies and all our affairs stems from our ability to attune with the concept; As above, so below.

The word disease stems from the word, ease, which denotes harmony. Disease is lack of harmony. Most illness stems from the ignorance, carelessness, stress or wilfulness of the individual. To the degree that we can discipline ourselves to correct habit patterns, we will be able to control our affairs with some degree of well-being.

In gaining a little deeper knowledge of numbers and astrology, one can enrich the life, and, beat the monotony of a humdrum existance. We all will experience, from time to time, peaks and troughs of the emotions and attitudes. But, by being able to familiarize ourselves with the planetary symbols, signs and numerical values, we can be more selective. Every facet of our life is governed by the phrase; As above, so below. In the matter of health, only a few hints will be given in this work.

Never cut on any part of the body, which is governed by the astrological sign related to it, when the Moon is transiting that sign. Healing will be found to be more difficult, especially if the Moon is in adverse aspect, square or opposition, to Mars, Saturn, Uranus or Neptune. For best results in a cutting operation, select a day when the Moon is increasing in light and making favorable aspects to the Sun, Venus, Mercury or Jupiter, and, posited in a sign other than that ruling the part of the body which is ailing. If a favorable date is selected, the operation should be successful and the healing swift.

Never use stimulants when ill when the Moon is near the full and conjoined to Mars. If in the case of emergency, this becomes necessary, considerable less dosage should be used.

Never use sedatives or depressants when ill when the Moon is in the last quarter, decreasing in light, when conjoined to Saturn. If in the case of an emergency this becomes necessary, considerable less dosage will be found to suffice.

When consulting a doctor about any particular condition, always try to select a day that is favorable. This would be a day when the Moon is increasing in light and making favorable aspect to the Sun, Venus, Mercury or Jupiter. Another *must,* in any consideration, is to make sure that Mercury, the planet of communication, is well aspected and *direct* in motion.

Right here we should note that of all aspects encountered in the astrological application, the direct Mercury is a *must.*

There are three times a year, for about three weeks, that Mercury turns retrograde. All the planets are always in direct motion all the time, but, the earth in relation to the other planets in its orbit around the Sun, experiences this retrograde motion in relation to the other planets due to the different paths around the solar orb. When Mercury is in this so-called retrograde motion in relation to the earth, only the routine and the necessary should be performed. Never try to force an issue or try to undertake a new course of action under a retrograde Mercury. Mercury rules communication and transportation. These factors are the most paramount in all our everyday transactions, and, are involved in all the facets of our lives.

A classic example that comes to mind that everybody should be able to remember, in regard to a retrograde Mercury, was our first astronaut in orbit. There are times when we do not control events, but, the events tend to control our affairs.

Around the first of February in 1962, the U.S. government announced that the first American astronaut was ready to be put into orbit. At the time, I was quite concerned because Mercury was retrograde. During the next few weeks each count-down was postponed. Five times the take-off was postponed. Mercury's number is (5). On the 19th of February Mercury went direct in motion in relation to the earth's orbit around the Sun. On February 20th, off went our astronaut into (3) orbits around the earth. It is of interest to note that the astronaut's name was, Glenn, (5) letters. He made (3) orbits around the earth, and, Mercury rules the (3rd) angle of the zodiac. It was done on the 20th, (2) plus (0) equals (2) day in the (2nd) month of 1962, (1) plus (9) plus (6) plus (2) which adds to (18), or (9) year. The Moon, numbers (2) and (7) which total to (9), was in Mercury's sign Virgo, an earth sign with a (5) value. Mercury, value (5), was conjoined to Mars, value (9), in Aquarius, an air sign.

Another example of a retrograde Mercury comes to mind when the Solano County Fair, in California, opened one summer before a record crowd of over 15,000 race fans. There had been quite a controversy over the racing dates for the Fourth of July, which had previously been assigned to the Alameda County Fair event. This particular year so much pressure was brought to bear by the Vallejo interests, that the Solano County Fair finally won out. Horse racing being one of my interests, found me at the track on that day. Being a frequent race goer, this was a routine affair for me. Everything seemed to be going smoothly for such a large crowd at such a small track, until the 5th race. Right at that time, a delay was caused by a power outage. The track management tried to punch out the mutual tickets by hand. (Mercury, number (5), rules the hands.) The break-down was so complete that the management had to close down the track operations and turn away the huge crowd. They were unable to run the fifth race.

We might note that the cause of the debacle was power, (5) total letters. This power is symbolized by the Sun, numbers 1 and 4 which total (5). This body rules the (5th) angle of the zodiac which governs this speculative sport. All this happened at the time of the fifth race.

One might say that these were unusual events, and, that one or two instances do not make a rule. The writer has had considerable experience with Mercury retrograde, and, I will add some more data for further insight, so that the readers may check it and judge for themselves. A lot of wasted time and money can be saved during the Mercury retrograde periods.

I might add that the author has a well aspected Mercury in the natal chart. So, one cannot say that this is an individual experience. But, it probably is to be my experience to get this message across to others for a better understanding of the astrological science. By the time the readers finish this book, they will have a better insight to the subject, which, can be used to greater advantage in their every-day lives.

The effects of a retrograde Mercury are not always felt during the three week periods while the planet is in this motion in relation to the earth. The total effect of such action taken under a retrograde Mercury may last months, and, even years. Mercury is the closest planet to the Sun, and, it has considerable influence over the mental faculties. So, one's decisions made during these periods of retrograde motion become very important. As I have said before, the routine and the necessary always should be the general procedure during these retrograde periods.

After World War (2), many folks had quite a time adjusting to civilian life. I, myself, had been shuffled around quite a bit, like most other folks, and, for reasons beyond my control. But, with the war behind us in 1947, I decided to try to get things under control. I decided that with my previous experience in banking and finance, I would like to try employment in Hawaii. Mercury was starting to slow down to go into retrograde motion during the latter part of June. It wasn't to be retrograde until July 2nd. So, I thought that I could start the ball rolling during the latter part of June.

I left my wife behind to clear up the loose ends and took off for the Islands to file my application with the Bank of Hawaii. I was told that my prospects were good for employment, but, my references would have to be checked and verified. My wife arrived after July 2nd with Mercury retrograde. I had not heard from the bank, so, we just took in all the islands and were having quite a time. About two days before Mercury went direct, my wife was on the beach playing with a youngster, when, all of a sudden, her back gave her considerable pain. She had been in traction months before, so, this was a reoccurrance of an old injury. She was told that an operation was necessary. Well, right then, we decided to return to the main-land for the surgery. Mercury went direct a couple of days later. The bank phoned for me to come to work. I had to cancel everything and booked passage back to California.

My wife had the surgery and I was job hunting again. Toward the end of October Mercury was slowing down again for the retrograde motion, when I landed a good job with the Trans-Arabian Pipe Line Co.; with their headquarters in Beirut, Lebanon. They had promised to try to bring the families out later if all worked out O.K. Well, Mercury went retrograde, and, the first Palestinian war broke out. The company spent about $50,000,000.00 and did not lay a foot of pipe. After about ten months, I was offered work in Kuwait or a completed contract. I decided on a completed contract and returned to California. I had a nice trip home visiting a lot of Mediterranean ports, but, by the time that my ship arrived in New York, Mercury had turned retrograde. My wife was waiting in New York to meet me, but, we missed connections. She had accepted a position in California and was sent to New York for training. Her firm needed her in California before my ship arrived. I booked a first class flight on United Air Lines back to San Francisco. First class was a misnomer. During the war years, and, right after the war, planes were literally flying their wings off without adequate servicing. We had flames shooting out over the wings from the motors from New York to Chicago. They tried to work on the engines, but, we ended up on a slower plane and arrived in San Francisco after a five hour delay. All this was under a retrograde Mercury.

Well, it was nice to be back in familiar surroundings again. After a nice two month vacation, I was ready to go back to the work routine. In the middle of October of 1948 Mercury was retrograde again. I was aware now of this astrological aspect, and, I proceeded with caution. I would do the routine and the necessary only. Well, the first thought was to go to an employment agency and fill out an application. I could get interviewed and sit back and wait for the action. The chap at the agency took one look at the application and said that I should go over and be interviewed at a local loan company. Well, I thought that to be quite routine, so, over I went. When I met the manager of the loan company, he turned out to be one of my wife's relatives. He insisted that I should come to work right then, and, that he would make my effort worth my while. Well, I finally gave in, and it all seemed very well, except that I did get stuck with the agency fee. I must say I was quite happy there. It looked like I had it made, as the expression goes. But, I was not aware that a retrograde Mercury could have prolonged effects. Three years later, out of the blue, the owners of the loan company decided to go out of business. Well, that was enough for me. The next time that I went job hunting I waited for a direct Mercury, and, good aspects. It did pay off. My next position was with a utility company and lasted twenty three years, right up to retirement. Should we note that the (2) plus the (3) totals to our (5)?

From here I shall leave it up to the readers to research these effects and aspects further, if they so desire.

Chapter 5
Geographical Zodiac

In this chapter we shall try to show the astrological relationships between the heavens, our zodiac, and the earth. Geographical astrology can be traced through the records preserved and handed down to us from the Greeks and Egyptians.

It is written that in the 5th century B.C., Herodotus visited Egypt. The priestly hosts showed him through a great hall, or, rotunda, in which were arranged in an unfinished circle (341) pironis, — (heroic wooden figures of men). He was told that they represented the generations of Egypt to Sethon, who ascended the throne (720) B.C.

In the chronology of Egypt, a lifetime is (72) years, or, the period of years that it took the solar orb to move (1) degree in the precession of the equinoxes. A generation was a half of a degree, or, (36) years. A complete circle equaled (360) degress. So, (19) more generations after Sethon would complete the circle. This coincided exactly with the year A.D. (0). It is of interest to note, before Sethon, (340 x 36) equals (12,240) years, and, from Sethon to A.D. (20 x 36) equals (720) years. When we add (12,240) to the (720) years we get the total of (12,960) years. This figure represented the total (360 x 36) Egyptian generations.

In its backward, or, western motion in the zodiac, referred to as precession, the Vernal, or, spring equinox, moved from Aldebaran through the first point of Aries, and, entered Pisces coincident with the birth of the Christian era. It is claimed that at that moment the signs and constellations of the zodiac coincided. It was celebrated as the New Year of the great Solar cycle of (25,920) years.

This great event occurred at (11) degrees of West longitude from Greenwich. This is the point that the solar orb begins its great circle around the zodiac. This point is known as (0) degrees of Aries, the beginning of the first astrological sign of the zodiac. Each (30) degrees to the east marks the beginning of another zodiacal sign, until we circle the globe, and, end with Pisces rulership over the Atlantic Ocean. From pole to pole, north to south, the same longitudinal degree of rulership governs.

In reflecting upon our geographical rulerships, we might note that Egypt falls under Taurus, symbolized by the bull. It is said that in those days wealth was measured by the possession of livestock, and, at one period, Egypt worshipped the Golden Calf. Aries covers most of Europe, and, this sign is said to be ruled by Mars, God of War. The history of Europe was greatly influenced by its wars. The Atlantic Ocean is ruled by Pisces, a water sign. Capricorn falls over the United States. The tenth angle of the zodiac, Capricorn, indicates leadership. Surely the United States is the most authoritative in world leadership. Scorpio and Sagittarius become adjacent signs along the west coast of the United States. Fire and water make steam. Scorpio, a water sign, and Sagittarius, a fire sign, make the U.S. west coast noted for its fogs. We might also note that Taurus, the natural 2nd angle of the zodiac falls over most of the Arab countries. The second angle of the zodiac rules money and possessions. Surely, some of those Arabs are some of the richest people of the world. Also under this angle of geographical rulership we find the Union of South Africa. This is another prosperous and wealthy group of people. Oil, Gold, and Diamonds are surely some of todays most valuable assets.

Geographical astrology has many benefits to offer all earthlings. One may voluntarily select a location that may be more favorable to the best aspects in one's astrological chart. Fire, Air, Earth and Water, the four triplicities of our zodiac govern personalities as well as geography and we may benefit accordingly. Any good astrologer can match an individual chart, (As above, So below), for the maximum beneficial results concerning health, wealth and happiness by using the geographical process described in this book.

In geographical astrology we can also afford ourselves the

opportunity to pinpoint areas of the earth receiving adverse directions from the zodiac. Storms, droughts, floods and earthquakes are all nothing more than magnetic stress points caused by the Sun, Moon and planets in their relationship to the earth's surface. Temperature changes in the air and water of only a few degrees in certain areas can make for considerable weather variations. There are many astrological books on this subject. Sun spots also are causes for many changes. Earthquakes are always the result of heavy adverse aspects between the slower moving planets and the Sun and the Moon. Parallels, squares and oppositions are always in effect during major earthquakes, and, we have noted how our geographical zodiac can pinpoint the magnetic action.

If our astronomers and weather forecasters were as open-minded as our N.A.S.A. officials, much more accurate earthquake predictions could be made, not to mention storms, floods and droughts. In chapter (13) of this book, which covers superstition, accidents and fate, the author has given a few clues as to how this may be accomplished.

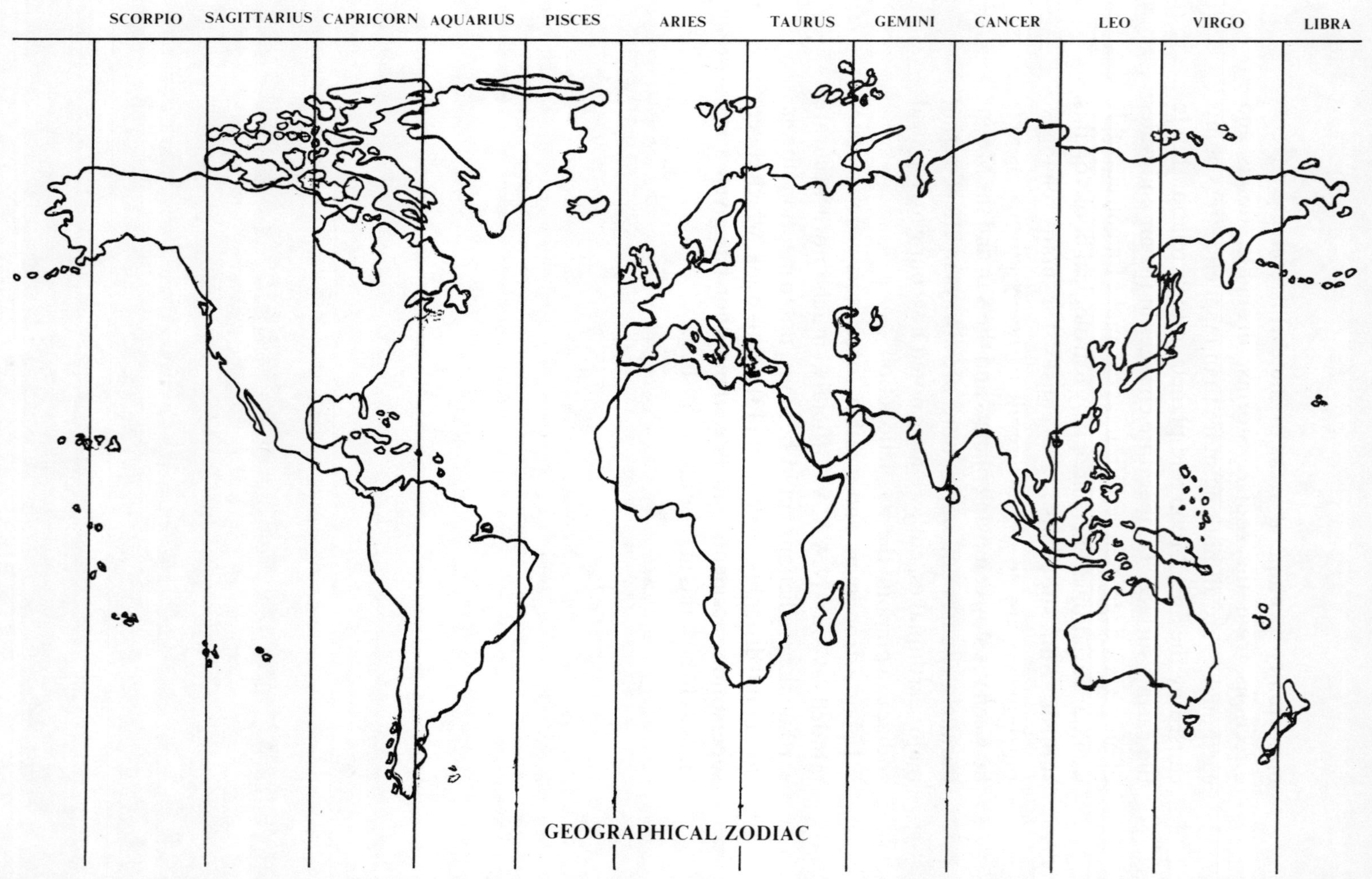

SCORPIO   SAGITTARIUS   CAPRICORN   AQUARIUS   PISCES   ARIES   TAURUS   GEMINI   CANCER   LEO   VIRGO   LIBRA
GEOGRAPHICAL ZODIAC

Chapter 6
English Cabala

At this point in this book we are now going to invite the readers to indulge in some very original, but, far-out learning. The ancient Hebrews and Egyptians used a cabalistic key to correlate the vibratory sounds in their alphabets to the signs and planets in the zodiac. There is enough written on the number value of their alphabets and sounds, but, when it is translated to the English, something was lost. One can still total the number of letters in words and arrive at a total value that can be used to correlate to the zodiacal values, and, this application is quite effective. However, the phonetic values are an added extension, and, in some instances, give a better picture and are much more effective.

The theory which the author has found to be very factual, maintains that when the heavens, the zodiac, show certain aspects and signs to be indicative of an event to take place, the corresponding numbers will be found to match in the name of the individual, animal or thing that completes the action on earth. This theory also postulates that when a question is asked, the answer is shown at the same time.

At first-hand it appears that one would have to be psychic to grasp this process. Perhaps one does develop one's intuitive faculties in the process. But when this is done with numbers, correlated to the planetary values, which can be identified by numbers, it is like a simple problem of addition.

First I will list the phonetic values for the English alphabet as proven correct through years of personal experience. Then I will list the dates, aspects and events so that the readers will be able to grasp the application used in the remaining chapters of this book.

Letter	Single Phonetic	Number Value	
A	ay	1	This is always a (1) value, short or long.
B	bee	3	The short sound of (B), as in (B)all is given a (2) value.
C	see	7	The short sound of (C), as in (C)an is given a (2) value.
CH	cha	8	The soft sound of CH, as in (CH)arlotte is given a (3) value.
D	dee	5	The short sound of (d), as in (D)an is given a (4) value.
E	ee	1	This is always a (1) value, short or long.
F	ef	9	(F) as in Frank is always an (8) value. (F) as in Of is a (6) value.
G	gee	4	(G) as in garage has two different sounds. The first (G) is the hard sound and is given a (2) value. The second (G) is the soft sound and is given a (3) value. The (E) in this word would be silent with no value given to it.
H	aach or aych	9	(H) as in (H)and is given an (8) value.
I	aye	1	This is always a (1) value, short or long.
J	jay	4	(J) as in John is given a (3) value.
K	kay	3	(K) as in Kiss is given a (2) value.
L	el	4	(L) as in Long is given a (3) value.
M	em	5	(M) as in Mine is given a (4) value.
N	en	6	(N) as in None is given a (5) value.

Letter	Single Phonetic	Number Value	
O	oh	6	(O) as in No is given the long sound of (6) (O) as in Or is given the short sound of (2) value.
P	pee	9	(P) as in Pie is given a (8) value.
Q	keyou	9	(Q) as in Quick is given a (2) value.
R	are	3	(R) as in Rank is given a (2) value.
S	ess	7	(S) as in Sink is given a (6) value.
T	tee	5	(T) as in Tank is given a (4) value.
U	you	7	(U) as in Blue is given a (6) value. (U) as in Blur is given a (2) value.
V	vee	7	(V) as in Victor is given a (6) value.
W	double-you	9	(W) as in Will is given a (6) value.
X	exs or axe	9	(X) is always (9) if not silent.
Y	why	7	(Y) in By or Yes is given a (1) value.
Z	zee	8	(Z) as in Zim's or Zebra is given a (7) value.

Other Sounds

SH a soft sound as in Ship is given a (3) value.

PH as sounded in Pheasant has an (F) sound as in Frank and is given an (8) value.

TH as sounded in This or Thin is given a (9) value.

OO as sounded in Boom is given a (6) value.

(J) as in San Jose is sounded as an (H) and given an (8) value. AU sounded as awe is given a (2) value. In the word or name Joaquin we would sound as waukeen, and, we would add 6 plus

2 plus 2 plus 1 plus 5 for a total of (16) or (1) plus (6) equals (7) phonetic total. Here we have given the (J) a (6) value for the (W) sound and oa a (2) value as sounded in AU. The (Q) is given the (2) value as in Kiss. The two (E)s are sounded only as one, so, we give them a value of (1). When we have a word or name where one or sometimes two letters are not sounded, we omit the values and do not count those letters. Where we have two letters with the same sound, we only count one value. An example would be as in Bill. This would total to (2) plus (1) plus (3) to a total of (6) phonetic total. The (B) is (2), the (I) is (1) and only one (L) is given the (3) value. The other is silent.

With a little practice one can become quite proficient in this application, as you can see from the following.

Using the word Communist, we get a total of (9) letters. In the phonetic we would sound this word as Com-u-nist and add 2 plus 2 plus 4 plus 7 plus 5 plus 1 plus 6 plus 4 to a total of (31). We then add to a single digit. (3) plus (1) equals (4) total phonetic value.

While we are counting values and letters, a little interpretation might help develop the intuitive skills. In this word communist, we have a (9) lettered word. This is the number of Mars. It is symbolical of aggressiveness, competitive and violent at times. The phonetic (4) total is the negative number of the Sun. It is symbolical of the cube or square. An adverse power aspect symbolizing effort or work. It is the builder's symbol with a powerful materialistic base. So, one might say that the word communist symbolizes negative leadership based on purely materialistic values in the name of humanity, (9) being a symbol of human values. It is also aggressive, domineering and violent.

In looking at the world map printed in English we find printed over the map of the Russian area; Union of Soviet Socialist Republics. This is supposed to be their official name. In applying our English cabala we come up with the following.

Union, (5) letters, Of, (2) letters, Soviet, (6) letters, Socialist, (9) letters and Republics, (9) letters. In adding we have 5 plus 2 plus 6 plus 9 plus 9 which totals (31) or (3) plus (1) equals (4) total letters for this name. Phonetically we add 2 plus 8 plus 6 plus 3 plus 9 which totals to (28) or (2) plus (8) equals (10) or (1) plus (0) equals (1). So the communists have a national identity which totals (4) letters and a phonetic value of (1). When we add the (4) plus the (1) we total to a (5) value. This is the Mercury value of transportation and communication. They do live up to their symbols by always being aggressive, competitive, materialistic and violent. They also try to export or transport their communist doctrine by every means and especially through propaganda. The phonetic value is the number (1) image that they continually strive for on all fronts. However, the total value (5) is somewhat neutral in that it is colorless without other planetary support. This is very evident in the manner that these communists try to use other folks to further their own ends.

The antithesis of communist is the word, capitalist. When we consider the total letters, they add up to (10) or (1). This number (1) is individualistic number of the first water. It is power supreme. First and foremost in power is the almighty dollar. It makes the wheels of industry roll. The United States, when looking at the world map and matching the heavens (zodiac) to the earth below, we find from our previous notations that Capricorn, the (10th) angle of the zodiac, which symbolizes power and authority plus prestige, falls directly over the United States. United, (6) letters, States, (6) letters adds (6) plus (6) equals (12) or (3), net for the total letters. Phonetically we have United (4) States (3) which totals to (7). When we add the (3) plus the (7) we total to (10) or (1). We are a capitalist nation with all that that entails. Number (6) is Venus number, and, Venus rules the second angle of the zodiac, which rules money and possessions. Double (6) nets to (3). This is Jupiter's number of growth and expansion. Here in the United States, money makes money. The (6) and the (3) are considered the money planets of the zodiac. We are the most prosperous nation on the face of the earth. The phonetic value of the word capitalist totals to a (4). This is also the builder's symbol of the square or the cube. It is a negative power number. A materialistic influence, but, a solid structure base. The number (7), the total phonetical value of the United States, is the full

Moon number. In Astrological lore the Moon rules the masses. Surely the United States symbolizes the fullness of the growth principal of the total letters, the (3) value, for the masses of its population. We have also noted that Jupiter, value (3), rules the (12th) angle of our zodiac, that of limitation. So, we do have definite limits to our present assets as indicated by the present world-wide energy crisis.

Between these two nationalistic giants, United States and Russia, the growing power struggle has resulted in a recognition of these limitations. Detent has entered the picture. Before analyzing the word, detent, I suppose that we should consider the name Russia. Here we find another (6) lettered word linked to a phonetic total of (8) which, when added to the (6), gives us a net of (14) or (5). This is the same number of their official listing on the English world maps; Union Of Soviet Socialist Republics. This just adds weight to the description previously given and more. The (6) total letters in the name Russia linked to the (8) phonetic value indicates the lack of personal freedom in this country and its government. Venus, value (6), is also considered ruler of personalities, or, personality as well as possessions and money. Saturn, value (8), is that of limitation and karma.

Getting back to our word, detent, we find that it has a total of (6) letters, and a total of (1) for the net phonetic value. When we add the (6) plus the (1) we total to (7). Both countries seek the first position (1) by continued manifestation of their way of life. The (6) letters denotes the perfect balance of the (2) equilateral triangles of the perfect (6) pointed star described in the previous chapter. Venus is the planetary value (6), that of harmony and balance. This body also rules the (2nd) angle of our zodiac, that of money and possessions. It also rules the (7th) angle, that of partnerships. So, the total (7) seeks the fullness of the (7th) house rulerships in that the desire is to avoid conflict, which is also governed by this angle, and, promote harmony between these two countries. Our Webster's dictionary defines, detent as; to unbend, relax, stretch or that which unlocks movement. Each country seeks continued growth of its own philosophy of government, which each thinks to be the best.

In the foregoing word and name analyzations I have tried to give some clues and insight as to just how this cabala does work. In the following chapters we shall continue this process. The word Russia, is a good example of our phonetic value application as it is counted 2 plus 2 plus 3 plus 1 which added to our (8). Note for the (ssi) we used the (SH) soft sound. Remember only what we sound, is that which should be added.

As a closing note to our chapter on Cabala we might mention that in our English alphabet we total (26) letters consisting of (5) vowels and (21) other letters considered as consonants. With these letters, or, symbols, we combine in various groups to form words to convey meaningful thoughts in structural form. We also use numbers (1) through (9) which can also be used in like manner in written form of words. The sounds enunciated in the different combinations of letters and numbers, or, words, total to (59) separate distinct variations. In our English cabala we correlate these sounds to our (7) planetary symbols through the use of simple numbers, (1) through (9).

It is of interest to note that the (59) adds (5) plus (9) to (14), or, (1) plus (4) to (5). This (5) value is our planetary symbol of Mercury. Mercury is our planetary communication symbol which is assigned rulership of the (3rd) angle, or, house of the zodiac which denotes amongst other things, speech, words and letters. Further, we can note that the word (vowels) shows a total of (6) for the letters and a phonetic total of (8). These two numbers total (6) plus (8) to (14), or, (1) plus (4) to *(5)*. The word (consonants) totals to (10), or, (1) for the letters and a phonetic net of (2). When we add the (1) plus the (2) we total to *(3)*. Remember Mercury, value *(5)* rules the *(3rd)* angle of our zodiac, that of communication. As above, so below — is clearly related in both the written and spoken words. Of course the total of (5) (vowels) and (21) (consonants) also bear witness to our Mercury (5) and (3rd) house rulership. If we continue our additions of the planetary value (5) plus its (3rd) rulership we total to an (8). This is our planetary value of Saturn which symbolizes form as well as our tenth angle rulership of the natural zodiac which in turn symbolizes the epitome of outward physical expression. Also, the total letters of our English language alphabet (26), or, (2) plus the (6) total to our (8). Again, As above, so below, — is clearly correlated.

Our words (English Alphabet) total to (15), or, (6) for the letters. The phonetic values total to a net of (8). When we add the (6) to the (8) we total to (14), or, (5), the symbol of Mercury which rules the (3rd) angle that of letters.

Writing and speaking are a form of creative expression. The most creative angle of our zodiac is the (5th) ruled by the Sun assigned number values (1) and (4). Further, the closest planetary body to the Sun is Mercury (5), our communication symbol.

Our English language cabala certainly does reflect our zodiacal symbols and rulerships. It is also truly creative and revealing.

Chapter 7
Space Age and Astrology

In the light of recent events in space, and, without becoming too involved in abstract discussion as to further reasons why things happen in the manner that they do, I would like to reflect upon some other events, which, when analyzed through the Astro-Numerical system, were interesting. So, if the readers will bear with me for a spell, hold tight and keep their cool, here it is.

In November of 1960, (a 7 year by our system), we had a presidential election in the U.S. On this day in November, the (11th) month which adds to (2) the other Moon value, Mercury, in astrological terms, was in retrograde motion in relation to our earth's motion.

This particular aspect, as we have noted before, is experienced about (3) times each year and lasts for about (3) weeks. We have also previously noted that this particular aspect tends to abort, delay or foul the normal process of communication, transportation and decision-making. The severity or strength of the aspect varies with closeness of the other aspecting bodies.

This was the election that put John F. Kennedy into the White House. A close count and charges of fraud and ballot tampering were made. Kennedy, (7) letters in his name, was elected in the (11th) month, which nets to (2), of a (7) year. (2) plus the (7) equals (9). John F. Kennedy was born in (1917), which nets to a (9). Nixon, (5) letters in his name, was defeated. Nixon was born in (1913), which nets to a (5), and, as we have noted, Mercury, value (5) was retrograde.

As we reduce all numbers to their single digits from (1) to (9), we can see from subsequent events how these two men were fated. Kennedy was a Gemini by birth and his Sun sign ruler was Mercury, value (5). Gemini is also the (3rd) angle of our zodiac. J.F. Kennedy died in his (3rd) year of his presidential term. Remember he was elected under a retrograde Mercury. The birth year, (1917), which adds to (9) is symbolized by Mars, value (9). This body is closely associated with violence under adverse aspects. The mode of Kennedy's death, by gun shot, is clearly indicated.

So, in recapping, we have Kennedy, (7) letters in his name, born on 5-29-1917 which adds to a net of (7) and dying on 11-22-1963 which adds to a net of (7).

It was Kennedy, (7) letters, born on the (29th) day which adds to a net of (2), who stated that the space program's objective was to put a man on the Moon, value (2) and (7).

This objective to put a man on the Moon was achieved. The name of the space craft was Apollo (11) or (2), the new Moon number. It took off on 7-16-1969. This is a (7) day, a (7) month and a (7) year. It landed on the Moon on 7-20-1969. This is a (2) day, a (7) month and a (7) year, or, — Blast off on a (7) day and Moon landing on a (2) day. (7) plus (2) equal (9). Two astronauts climbed down (9) steps to put their two feet on the Moon. The astronaut's suits were too stiff to allow the men to bend over to touch the Moon's surface.

Of the (7) planetary significators of the event, the (2) key factors were Uranus and Jupiter conjoined to the Moon in the (7th) angle of our zodiac, Libra, ruled by Venus, numerical value (6). The (2) astronauts were named, Armstrong, (9) letters, and Aldrin, (6) letters. (9) plus (6) total (15) or (6). The unusual scientific nature of this successful event was clearly indicated. The Moon was increasing in light and Mercury was in direct motion in relation to the earth. Uranus cycle is (7) years through one sign of the zodiac and it was conjoined to the success planet, Jupiter, on the cusp of the (7th) angle of the zodiac. From 1963, the year that Kennedy died, to 1969 is (6) years. Uranus, value (6), is the higher octave of Venus, value (6). From 2-20-1962, the date of the first man in orbit, Glenn (5) letters, to 7-20-1969 when the lunar landing took place, the interval is (7) years and (5) months to the day. — Remember Kennedy, (7) letters in his name and birth sign Gemini, Ruled by Mercury, value (5).

It is also worthy to note that the natural (7th) angle of the zodiac squares the (4th) angle of the zodiac, ruled by the Moon, values (2) and (7). The only complaint against the pioneering event came from those more interested in domestic progress and development, indicated by the (4th) angle affairs with Moon rulership.

Another tid-bit of prime importance during the Moon spectacular was that we had another Kennedy (7) letters making the news unfavorably on the domestic scene, (2) people in a car accident. The place, Chappaquiddick Island which adds to (20) or (2) total letters and another Moon value.

In spite of all the fanfare pertaining to this tremendous, scientific spectacular, the astronauts found the Moon to be a most inhospitable and foreboding place. The whole world prayed for their safe return. This singular space achievement tends to focus attention on the duality of all events and moods. So, when all the hurrahs were over, we had to look forward to more pressure for social progress and development.

In completing our reflections upon this event we should note that with all the most advanced computer data, there was an element of over-load for the mechanical gadgets that put the space craft off about (4) miles. The (4) is symbolical of the square aspect in the astrological lore and is considered negative or adverse. It was only the human element of courage, (7) letters, skill, (5) letters and will, (4) letters, that actually made the final touchdown, a success. Of course we must add the (7) plus the (5) plus the (4) to arrive at our (16) or our final (7). I suppose that one could say our side won by a score of (7) to (0), — the opposition being in this instance, the Russian space program.

We might also note that space is an extension of consciousness. The conditions and events that take place in space depend upon the growth of human consciousness, not on the amount of funds allocated to the space program. The infinitude of space is indicative of the infinite possibilities of growth for human consciousness.

Chapter 8
Baseballs and Planets

Six and then seven, that is a loser on the crap table. However, that can be a winning combination on the baseball diamond. Conjunctions between planets in the sky, according to the astrological science, can be quite powerful, along with eclipses and the like. But, just as potent are the conjunctions between bats and baseballs on the diamond at the ballpark to the baseball filberts.

For the interest of readers that are baseball fans, I have selected the date of September 22, 1969. A (9) month, a (4) day and a (7) year, which adds to (20), or, (2). This is the new Moon number and this date fell on a Monday, ruled by the Moon. The Moon rules the masses, or, general public. So, this date proved to be of interest to a lot of people, especially to the baseball buffs, and, more in particular, to the Giant fans.

During the month of September in 1969 we had (2) eclipses. One of the Sun and one of the Moon. We also had a period of retrograde Mercury. But, on this particular date the Sun was leaving Mercury's sign Virgo, and, about to enter the zodiacal sign of Venus, that of Libra. It was about to leave the natural (6th) sign of the zodiac and about to enter the natural (7th) sign of the zodiac. This sign Libra contained Jupiter (3), Uranus (6) and Mercury (5). On this day the Moon was transiting Aquarius, ruled by Saturn value (8). The Sun is the hour hand on our cosmic clock and the Moon is the second hand.

Around the time of the first eclipse, that of the Sun, a battery of news media laid siege to Candlestick Park in San Francisco, when, the one and only Willie Mays hit his 599th home run. When we add (5) plus (9) plus (9) we total to (23) or (5). This is Mercury's number. As we mentioned, Mercury went retrograde during this month, but, it was in good company conjoined to the Sun, Jupiter and Uranus. The retrograde Mercury had a tendency to delay the coming event, but, it did not prohibit it from maturing, mainly because of the potent planetary conjunctions and eclipses.

Willie Mays, (6) plus (4) letters in his name adds to (10) or (1). He certainly was a number (1) chap. Willie was born under the zodiacal sign of Taurus, value (6). This number (6) is the key to our event as the magic number 600, (6) plus (0) plus (0) equals (6). The key to the place where the event was to take place proved to be San Diego, (3) plus (5) letters which add to (8). Saturn, planetary value (8) was transiting Willie's Sun sign. Saturn's astrological influence, as we have mentioned, rules age and is shackling and restrictive. Willie was in his sunset years as an active player. On this particular evening, he was warming the bench. Not even in the game. So, we pick up our scene from here.

On September 22, 1969, in San Diego, on a balmy Monday evening, the Moon was riding high in the sky increasing in light and making favorable trine aspect to the (3) planets transiting the Venus sign Libra, value (6). The Giants, (6) letters, were leading the Padres, (6) letters, by a score of (2) to (1) going into the last half of the (6th) inning, when things began to jell.

Bryant, (6) letters in his name, was pitching for the Giants. With a count of (2) balls and (2) strikes on the batter, the pitcher injured himself. He threw one more pitch and had to leave the game. We can note that (2) plus (2) plus (1) adds to (5) and Mercury was retrograde. McMahan, (7) letters in his name, came on to pitch for the Giants. When the inning was over, the score was (2) to (2). In the action that took place in the (6th) inning, the Giants put in a player by the name of Foster, (6) letters in his name, for defensive purposes.

Opening the (7th) inning, Ron Hunt, (3) plus (4) letters in his name which total to (7), singled infield and was on first base. Foster, (6) letters in his name, was to bat next, but, out of the dugout, (6) letters in word dugout, came the man of the hour. None other than the number (1) chap, Willie Mays, remember (6) plus (4) letters add to our number (1). On the first pitch Willie sent the ball into orbit for Home Run, (4) plus (3) adds to (7), number (600), or (6) plus (0) plus (0) equals (6). This made the score (4) to (2) in favor of the Giants. This eventually turned out to be the final score (4) to (2) which also adds to our (6) value.

Willie hit his historic round-tripper off of Padre pitcher named Corkins, (7) letters in his name, in the top half of the (7th) inning on a Monday, ruled by the Moon values (2) and (7), and batted in (2) runs.

The top of the (7th) inning happened to be the Bonus Bonanza, (5) plus (7) adds to (3), inning of a radio sponsor. Jupiter, value (3) was posited in the natural (7th) angle of the zodiac ruled by Venus, value (6). These two values, or, planets are considered the money planets of the zodiac. This blow off the bat of Mays, (4) letters, hit on the (22nd), (2) plus (2) add to (4), won $2,200.00, which also nets to (4), for a man named George Kerker, (6) plus (6) nets to (3) letters in his name.

The Sun conjoined to Uranus usually brings about unusual things and oddities. Right after this event took place, the press box at the park received a phone call from a reporter in Fresno, (6) letters, telling Hodges and Simmons, the radio announcers that not only was the man who won the $2,200.00 from Fresno, but, also Foster, (6) letters, and Corkins, (7) letters, the man for whom Willie pinch-hitted and the man who threw the pitch, also were from Fresno. Also we might note that the name of the man who phoned George Cooper, (6) plus (6) letters in his name.

We can also note that the radio announcers, Hodges, (6) letters, and Simmons, (7) letters, were also part of the scenario that took place in the (6th) and (7th) innings of this historical game. Oh, yes, there is more —. The distance that the ball traveled to get out of the park was 391 feet, or (3) plus (9) plus (1) adds and nets to (4). This matches the (4) letters in the name of Mays. The manager, who pulled all the strings was named King, (4) letters. On the back of the man who trotted home in front of Willie, Ron Hunt, was the big number (33), or, (3) plus (3) adds to (6). To be sure, on the back of Willie Mays, the star of the show, was old number (24), which of course is (2) plus (4) giving us our biggest and final (6).

Chapter 9
Character and Numbers

In this chapter we shall delineate a bit on the different numbers and their personal uses and characteristics. We have indicated through our symbol descriptions, how dates and names and all earth phenomenon are inter-related, — As above, so below.

It has been noted by the author, that the daily events in the news can also be associated with the numerical value of that day and the aspects between the planets and signs of our zodiac.

The first day of the year, the first day of the month and the first day of the week, all symbolize a beginning, or, a start. First come, first served, denotes preference. Number (1) is the individual number, very personal and symbolizes personalities. It denotes things of a primary nature. Important people, leaders and such things and events. When our calendars show the date to be the first, number (1) day of the month, these are the kind of people, things and events that we can expect to find in our major news stories for that particular day, especially if the zodiacal aspects agree. In personal lives, activities also tend to follow these patterns. This is a date that all people born on a (1) day should use for all their pet projects, or, major action. This would include all born on a (1), (10), (19), or (28) date, as we add all numbers to a final single digit, and, they are considered (1) day personalities.

When the calendar reflects a (2) day, which includes (2), (11), (20), and (29), personalities, events and news tend to deal with the domestic scene. This is especially so, if the Moon on these dates is increasing in light, going from new to full, and, is making strong aspects to the other planetary bodies in our zodiac. Usually events on a (2) day deal with the general public, or, the masses. It tends to bring individuals before the public, and, sometimes things not too clear, or, hidden are brought out into the open, or, considerable light is shed upon them. The Moon has considerable influence upon females, liquids, homes and home-life. Change in trends, a new tact, phase, or, something new to follow is characteristic of each phase, or, quarter of the lunar cycle. Public figures, popular personalities, monetary or financial reserves are additional factors that work their way into the news items on (2) days. These are dates that all people born on a (2) day will be drawn into action, either through their own efforts, or, through the efforts of others. If this (2) date happens to fall on a Monday all the foregoing should receive additional impetus.

Number (3), which includes (12), (21) and (30), is a growth number. These people seem to have all their affairs and activities enlarged or expanded on these dates. Instrumental or group activities, relatives, churches, clubs, government, elected officials, judges, universities, foreign countries, shipping, foreign trade and all personnel connected with these activities tend to make the news. All (3) numbered people should select these dates for their action dates. When Thursday falls on a (3) day, these people and all the activities mentioned above receive additional power.

As a personal example, the author played golf on a small nine hole par (3) course recently. It was in the (3rd) month of March, on a (3) date which fell on a Thursday. The Sun on this day was making a favorable aspect to Jupiter, value (3). I had one of my best days and shot (2) rounds in the low (30's). On the fourth hole, I almost had a hole-in-one, the ball stopped 1/3rd of an inch from the edge of the cup. While walking down the fairway, I just happened to glance into the rough and found a new ball. Of course, it had a number (3) on it. All this happened on my third round of play for that week, on that particular course.

Number (4), including (13), (22) and (31) is the negative number of the Sun. In contrast to number (1), also a Sun number which is indicative of beginnings, this number (4) symbolizes function, such as a builder or a process of building. It is the number of organization, foundation and structure. As number (1) indicates beginnings the number (4) symbolizes endings. It is a materialistic factor, practical and denotes natural resources, mineral rights, such as oil and water, coal and etc. Number (1) indicates leaders and number (4) indicates builders and organizers. On (4) dates these people and things usually make the news. When we mention, things, we also mean all persons connected with these things or activities.

Throughout each month, the first (4) numbers that we have described, in a (31) day month, each have (4) days for action dates. The remaining numbers (5) through (9) only have (3) days for action dates. So, in some degree, we have authority, Sun, popularity, Moon, and opportunity, Jupiter, shown as more desirable numbers, especially in name considerations.

Number (5) is our middle number and dates (5), (14) and (23) tend to indicate communication, transportation, publication, accounting and education. Also clerks, agents, representatives, authors, editors, reporters and children are strongly influenced and indicated by this number (5). This is Mercury's number and the news media in general; periodicals, newspapers, radio, T.V., movies and etc; are all under the influence and direction of this planetary body. When Mercury (5) is well aspected and in direct motion, news can be informative and accurate. When Mercury (5) is in retrograde motion, even the necessary and routine is an effort to work out. When Mercury is retrograde and adversely aspected, (5) numbered birthdays should be especially cautious. This is the period that major foul-ups or errors are made.

Number (6), which includes (15) and (24) is considered a money number. All possessions, wealth, including clothes, furs, jewelry and food stuffs, fall under the influence of this number of Venus, (6). It is considered negative, feminine and sociable. Health, work and service all contribute to monetary measurement and fall under the influence of this number. It is considered artistic, graceful and strongly influences all the arts and crafts. When this number identifies the calendar day and the aspects are generally favorable, it is an excellent time for planning social amusements of all varieties. Love affairs prosper under these directions and all these items make the news on a (6) day when the aspects indicate through zodiacal action. These are the days most favorable for (6) numbered people, or, people with strong (6) value aspects.

Number (7) which includes (16) and (25), is a full Moon number. When the two lights, the Sun and the Moon, are (6) signs apart in the zodiac we have a full Moon period. It is considered a lucky number as it tends to bring all activities to fulfillment. It denotes all forms of partnerships. It is a legal influence as it brings others into focus as related to the self. It is a positive number which tends to work out through public activities. Usually things started at the new Moon period are brought to a head at the full of the Moon, or, a culmination of a phase of the activity is achieved. These are good days for (7) numbered people to select for their best action. These (7) numbered people are usually well balanced, good natured and popular folks interested in the welfare of others.

Number (8), including (17) and (26), is a karmic number. It is associated with age and limitation. Work and effort are also associated with this number. In a sense this is a money number that does have considerable financial influence over estates, legacies, taxes and insurance. The (8th) angle of the zodiac which governs these affairs also is the rulership of the marriage partner's finances. It is not considered as fortunate but more as a fateful influence. It is associated with destiny. On this numbered date, besides all the above, old or chronic problems tend to make the news, along with other partnership finances and divorce settlements. Tradition, custom and procedure usually favor these (8) numbered people, and they usually have great staying power and experience. These (8) numbered dates are best for their activities.

Number (9), including (18) and (27), is a date indicative of action, usually too much action. This number is often associated with force and violence. Fires also are under the influence of this number. Individuals who have this number for a birthday are usually forceful, active and sometimes impatient, both with the self and others. Tempers, angry words, quarrels and threats are inclined to be experienced on a number (9) date. Number (9) birthdays can use this number (9) date constructively if they can keep the cool, but, they can also get burned if they lose their cool. On (9) days the news can be quite violent and destructive, yet, on other days under good aspects a lot of active accomplishment can be noticed.

Each individual reflects the nature of the number of the date on which they are born. On these same numbered dates in each month, one should be able to put them to good use.

The full date of birth, month, day and year, added to a single digit is a fateful number of destiny. It is another number that cannot be changed. For good, or, ill we will experience it. To understand this number fully, one must correlate it to the zodiacal equivalent and note its aspects in one's natal chart. If this total date matches the individual birthdate, the actual day on which one is born, it gains in power, but remains limited in scope. When a different number than the birthday is totaled, the individual tends to experience a greater scope of activity. Whether this is good or ill, depends on the aspects to that corresponding planetary value's aspects in the natal chart.

Our parents usually give us our names, other than the surname, and, they also are not of our choice. However, they can be changed, even the surname can be changed. These given names reflect personality more than destiny. Our friends and others identify us by them. Subconsciously we take on a picturization of the sum total of the letters and phonetic value of the letters in our name. If our lives have been fortunate and we have experienced popularity, health, wealth and happiness, we no doubt have our name totals match a number symbol that is reflected favorably in our natal chart. A suggested change would not be desired. But if our lives to date have been anything but pleasant and feel like we would like to improve our lot, well, it can be done. We not only can change our name to a more favorable number symbol indicated by our natal chart, but, we can also select a more favorable location for our residence and activities. So, by the foregoing, the readers can take it from here. Any good astrologer can assist one to do this. This can be done for the basic natal chart or can be done temporarily for the progressed chart.

A case in point would be as protection for a witness in a

criminal court action. This is done quite often, though I doubt through astrological advice. But, many public figures and show people, by just a different spelling, adding or dropping a letter or two, have helped their image, health and fortunes.

The events that transpire from day to day are primarily governed by the major aspects transpiring in the zodiac on that particular day. They tend to vary in power by the increase or decrease of the lunar light. When the nature of the aspect above can be identified with the number and date of the calendar on earth, the items in the news for that particular day will reflect accordingly. So, if the birth number of the individual be so matched then that person will also experience similar activity.

In consideration of the solar and lunar periods or cycles, we find that individuals, events and things can experience expanded fields of magnetic power.

The Sun represents the hour hand on our cosmic clock and its influence is of prime significance. The Sun takes about (30) days to transit (1) zodiacal sign. Its numbers, (1) and (4), refer to both the (1) yearly cycle, and the (4) seasonal effects. Everybody seems to respond to these influences whether they are aware of them or not. The (30) day cycle is something else. People that are actively involved in life, and that includes most of us, can appreciate knowing that when the Sun by transit is in our own zodiacal sign, it favors all of our activities. When the Sun by transit reaches our birthday, then this is our strongest magnetic period. The Sun literally shines upon us. We usually feel better, are more optomistic, which in turn effects and favors all of our activities. These favorable periods are also experienced, maybe to a slightly less degree, when the Sun is transiting any other sign of the same triplicity, as that of our Sun sign. Such as a fire sign is favorable to the other fire signs. The same goes for the air, earth and water triplicities.

When the Sun, by transit, reaches a sign that is (90) degrees removed from our Sun sign, it is a time to exercise caution. This is also the rule when the Sun, by transit, reaches the opposition, (180) degrees, to our Sun sign. During the (90) and (180) degree aspects we tend to feel at cross purposes and opposed to the general trend of events and things that we experience. These are usually periods that call for all our talents just to see us through. Any good astrological text will help acquaint the reader with these yearly dates.

The Moon is considered the second hand on our cosmic clock. It circles the zodiac in about (27) days. When this body is, by transit, in one's own Sun sign, then these days become favorable, for on these days, we are more magnetic and attuned to all that is happening around us. We have about (2) and a half days of this transit in which to push our pet projects. If the Sun cycle and the lunar cycle and the birthdate number match, then this becomes a date that should be especially favorable, for all our activities. The Moon, by transit, also makes the (90) and (180) degree aspects. The (90) degree square aspect is experienced (7) days after the Moon leaves the Sun sign. The (180) degree opposition occurs (7) days after that square aspect. Then (7) days after the opposition aspect we experience another (90) degree square aspect. Then the cycle is repeated. While making this complete cycle, the Moon, like the Sun, makes the favorable (120) degree trine aspect each time that it transits the triplicity sign. So, (9) days after leaving our Sun sign, the Moon will favor our activities for about (2) and a half days. Also, (18) days after leaving our Sun sign is another (2) and a half day favorable period.

In a cycle of about (27) days, our emotions and affairs are favorably influenced for about (7) and a half days. Then for about (7) and a half days the reverse is true. The other days are considered about average. We must also remember that things and events that get started around the time of the new Moon period tend to gain in activity up until the full Moon period and then they tend to lull or recede. If we can gage our affairs to go with this flux we will find that the momentum will be to our advantage.

With just these few notes regarding the Solar and Lunar cycles, together with our birthdates, we have ample information to enrich our lives in numerous ways.

Chapter 10
Gambling Casinos and Astro-Numerology

There is no activity that is influenced more, by numbers and their zodiacal symbols in the heavens, than the gambling casinos.

Before getting into a detailed analysis of Astro-Numerical values and gambling, it may be well to digress a bit and see if we know just what we are doing when we gamble.

Several years back, I read in the daily newspaper where a chap had leased rooms in the Marine Memorial Building in San Francisco for the showing of color films of bare hand psychic surgery. I had read many articles about psychic healing and have four or five books on the subject in my personal library. In fact, when the doctor told my mother that she would just have to live with her arthritic condition, that he could do nothing for her, I wrote to the famous Harry Edwards on her behalf. I had heard where Mr. Edwards filled Alberts Hall in London and gave public demonstrations before doctors and scientists on live television in England. Before I had received his reply by return mail, my mother had hung up her cane and was free from the arthritic condition for her remaining days.

I am aware that faith plays a major part in all spiritual healing, and, as we think, so we are. I have also seen people hypnotized perform super-human feats. Like needles run clear through their palms, like hat pins and with absolutely no pain, bleeding or trace of wound afterward.

I was one of the early arrivals and secured a good seat for the show. There was a short talk before the showing of the films. It seems that this chap, who's name I shall omit, was an ex-service man who had seen all this activity while he was on duty in the Philippine Islands during the war years. After the war he went back to the area to study and film what he had witnessed.

Thousands of people, mostly poor rural folks without any financial means, were operated upon every month. Also, many people with adequate financial means found their way to this psychic healer, who accepted nothing but offerings that one could afford. After the talk, the films were shown. It was hard to believe what I had seen. I was very impressed to say the least. Complete operations with no instruments, just bare hands to open, remove, close and heal without any evidence of pain or scars. Well, I did manage to purchase this chap's book and learned in considerable more detail about his connection and experience.

About a week later, I was invited to a residence of an acquaintance where a private lecture was given on this same subject, psychic healing. It was in Marin County, just north of San Francisco. After the lecture a little demonstration was given on the power of the subconscious mind. I was sitting in the front row for a clear view and easy hearing. The demonstration consisted of two people holding a four inch wide piece of adhesive tape about three feet in length very taut. The chap giving the demonstration was going to pass his hand through the four inch adhesive tape and break it clean like a knife. The way that he did this, was to think about what he wanted to do for about a minute. Then he looked away from the tape toward the clock in the room. He said that he did this to take his conscious mind off of what he was about to do. Then, — wham!, he passed his open hand right through the tape. No fraud, a perfectly honest demonstration. I was very impressed.

The conversation after that was about the same as any other home gathering until I mentioned some pictures that I had of some U.F.O.'s; unidentified flying objects. The chap, with whom I had been talking, was an electronic design engineer by profession. When I admitted that I had seen a U.F.O. over my home in Mill Valley, he said that was probably true, and, that if I was interested, that he could mentally have one over that residence in less than ten minutes. Well, I thought that I was talking to some kind of a nut for sure! The weather was clear and balmy that evening, so, when he invited us out into the patio for a try, well, I couldn't resist. Believe it or not, in less than five minutes this object, bright in the clear night sky, moved high overhead. To acknowledge and confirm this as a real U.F.O., he mentally had the object zig-zag directly overhead.

I mention this foregoing data simply to show the readers that there are things and forces all about us that we don't even imagine, let alone believe. The average person, when they think of gambling, assume that it is a process of pure chance. When one is confronted with a lottery, such as the military draft, or, a sweepstakes, such as the Irish sweepstakes, it is hard to discount luck or chance. Yet, there is no such thing as luck or an accident. So, lets digress a little further.

Throughout our United States today, there is much interest in the philosophies of the Far East countries. We have many folks becoming interested in meditation. This has come to pass partly because of the jet age. The world has become a much smaller place. Through the media of television and jet airplanes, more people have been sold on the tourist business, and, are travelling about visiting more countries. In so doing, they see how other people live and function. An exchange of students and culture has taken place. We have become aware that the caucasian race is much more developed along material scientific lines of so called progress, but, it is a minority in the world's population.

This development, or, advance in science and medicine has accelerated the pace of living in our western society. One might think that we should be free from want, fear and infirmities. Yet, today, we are building bigger and better hospitals and are so developed industrially that we are suffering from pollution problems. We seem to have more health problems proportionately to our industrial growth.

Through the inter-exchange of cultures these Eastern philosophies have taken hold in the West, mainly because we have a need for them. We have more people living better and having more productive lives because they have learned the Art of Meditation. The Art of Meditation is the art of release, release of tension caused by daily living. Some people experience more stress in the daily life than others. These people tend to reap more immediate benefits than others. But, once the art of perfect relaxation has been achieved, then all who practice the Art of Meditation begin to develop their inner powers. Better performance in their daily lives is usually their first beneficial experience. Then gradually E.S.P.; estra sensory perception, begins to be a noticeable factor in their lives. Once we become aware of these powers, then we are able to take dominion of our lives and vehicles and attune to the divine principle that governs all.

Now to get back to our next phase of numbers and planetary symbols in relation to the gambling casinos. Astrologically, gambling is a fifth (5th) angle activity, speculation, gambling, amusement and etc. This angle of the zodiac very aptly describes the affairs that one encounters when visiting the Nevada casinos.

Gambling, is an (8) lettered word with a phonetic value which totals to (2). When we total the (8) and the (2) we add to a (1). The (8) value would suggest limitation. All casinos have limits to the wagers and pay-offs. The (2) value indicates a popular public activity and the lunar influence on all gambling. The (1) is a Sun value and this body rules the 5th angle of the zodiac under which this activity falls. Casino, is a (6) lettered word with a phonetic value of (3). When we total the (6) and the (3) we add to a (9) value. The (6) indicates a popular social activity, also a money influence. The (3) value is a growth principal, also one of opportunity. The (6) and (3) are both money numbers and this is what makes for the name of the game. Of course the (6) added to the (3) gives us a (9) value. This is the value of Mars and shows a powerful force of desire. It is also the human number which would cover most individuals. When we add the total number for the word, gambling, to the total of the word, casino, (1) plus (9) we total (10) or (1). This we see is the Sun's number which rules this (5th) angle activity. The Sun is the symbol of prestige and power. Las Vegas is truly the gambling capital of the world. All the big shows, names and stakes eventually find their way to this spot. No doubt most of the readers have already been this route. This city is literally built around the gambling casinos.

As we have shown, the time of the Moon, to use an old phrase, is very important in such a venture. We can select a good period for ourselves if we learn to read our natal charts and the current ephemeris. In fact the daily newspapers can inform us as to the Moon's different phases. Also whether it is increasing in light or decreasing in light. By being able to select a favorable period for ourselves, we increase our ability to have a pleasant experience without losing our shirt.

There are a variety of games for the pleasure seekers. From the one-armed bandits and bingo to the roulette, craps, black-jack and keno, not to mention money wheels, poker and a few miscellaneous items like football pools and horse books. No matter which game is played, each is strongly influenced by the astro-numerical values from (1) through (9).

I suppose that one of the best descriptions of the astro-numerical function and use would be to quote from some personal experience with their uses.

Several years back, when I first became interested and aware of the astrological influences on gambling, I made several trips to the Nevada casinos to test what I had suspected. The best success was with horses and racing. But every operation in gambling responds like clockwork to the solar and lunar aspects.

The most popular game in Nevada gambling casinos is craps. We can note that craps is a (5) lettered name. As we have stated, value (5) is the number of the angle of the zodiac that governs this gambling activity. So, it is natural that the phonetic value of this name, craps adds to number (1). It is the number one game in all the casinos. The big money maker and prestige game, as indicated by the number of tables, space and personnel assigned to its operation. Note: (5) plus (1) totals (6) Venus (money).

In reviewing our numerical factors, we find that the number (7) seems to be the key to the game of craps. We have noted that the (7) is the full Moon number, and, that the Moon's influence waxes and wanes from week to week. It is strongest at the full and weakest at the last quarter, and, the so-called dark of the Moon, just before the new lunation.

There are (36) ways to make (11) numbers on the crap table. We can note that (3) plus (6) equal (9). These two numbers are the money numbers of our zodiac, (3) and (6). The (9) is the total of the Moon's values, (2) and (7). In the (3), (6), (9), associated numbers, the (6) is the middle number. It is the number (7) which can be made by (6) different combinations and is the easiest number to roll on the crap table. Also we can note that of the (11) numbers that can be rolled, (7) of them are in the field area on the table. The (11) or (2) is one of the field numbers.

We can deduce from the above, that when the Moon is well aspected, increasing in light, and Mercury, number (5), is in direct motion, the Moon's values, (2) and (7) should be quite active. So, by further deduction, we can note that at such a period, the (7), (6) ways to make, and the field, (16) ways to make, adds to (22) ways out of the (36) possible. This is about (61) percent in the player's favor. Note (6) plus (1) equal (7). We might as well mention that the (22) is a net of (4), and, the (4) and the (10) are in the field. The number (10) on the crap table is really our number (1), there being no other number (1) possible. These are the Sun's values. So, when the Sun and the Moon are strongly aspected, all the above gets more power, especially if the date matches our numbers and the individual's number value is one of them.

This is good information for the dice players. They can supplement their line play with field wagers.

Contrary to most books on craps, when the Moon is decreasing in light, or, in the dark of the Moon, one of the best spots on the crap table, after a (7) is rolled, is the Big (6) and (8). It does not lose until another (7) is rolled. I suppose that these numbers could be played direct with much better odds, but this is an easy spot for the novice. Action can get quite active and hectic around the crap table and the simpler one can play, the better. These two numbers are the next easiest numbers to make as there are ten ways in which they can be made. When one of these numbers is rolled, the process is to remove the wager until another (7) is rolled and the process can be repeated. One may not win every time, but, when the Moon is weak, cadent and decreasing in light, one can make it pay. Especially if one's birthdate number adds to (6) or (8) and the Sun and Moon in their sign.

I chose the period of the full Moon for my operation, and, it proved to be a real experience. I arrived at the north end of Lake Tahoe late at night. I made my first stop at the Cal-Neva Lodge on my way to Stateline at the sound end of the lake. I knew that the south end of the lake had much more activity, but, I thought that it might help to get started in a more relaxed atmosphere.

I walked up to the only table with any action, at that late hour, and, found only five or six people gambling, including a couple of drunks. I stood next to a sober chap and put a wager on the front line. I started while one of the drunks was rolling the dice. The point was made and then the drunk put a larger amount on the table. This time the point was (9). After a few throws the (9) was made. The head stick-man had his working stick-man move the marker to number (5). The drunks just kept rolling the dice. The chap standing next to me began to protest. But, the stick-man said that it was just a mistake in placing the marker. Well, the drunk rolled a (7) and lost his wad. The chap next to me blew his stack and they told him to blow if he didn't like the operation. It was obvious that something was not Kosher, so, I immediately left for the south end of the lake.

The south end of the lake was live and jumping, even at that late hour. The frenzy that can be generated at a crap table has to be seen to be believed. Despite all the noise and hilarity, I was doing O.K. —, winning. Finally one of the stick-men noticed that I had a method to my sequence. Right then I learned lesson number two. Never let a house person know or suspect that you have a method or system of play. I was given such a bad time that I finally had to leave. But, I had proved to myself that; As above, so below, will work if one can be selective.

The next time that I had a favorable solar and lunar period was on a three day week-end. This time I thought that I would try the Black Jack table. This was a quick and short experience. The total letters in the name Black Jack add to (5) plus (4) equals (9). This is Mars number which denotes force and aggressiveness. The phonetic values are (8) and (6) which total to (5). This number (5) is symbolical of the speculative nature of the game. The (8) number is that of Saturn and it denotes restrictions. The dealer has to stand on (17) or (1) plus (7) equals the (8). The (6) is a money number, but, when combined with the number (8) it nets to the (5). It is very speculative. Mercury is a mental influence and decision is the key to success in this game. It is also dual in nature and players are allowed to split pairs and play two hands. Hands are also ruled by Mercury, remember (5) digits on each hand.

My approach was simple, playing one hand, and, using my own judgment as to whether to hit or stand. It came to a shuffle period and the dealer showed the Queen of spades, which was burned or placed on the bottom of the deck face up. Then the cards were dealt, and, after all had decided to hit or stand, the dealer turned up a black-jack with an ace and the Queen of spades as the hole card. I wasn't too happy with that turn of events. Of course, I left the game, pronto.

A few weeks later, on some talk show on the television, I saw a demonstration given with cards. The chap just shuffled the cards well and then proceeded to deal himself four aces. Ever since that I have been cold to card games.

The word card has a total of (4) letters and a phonetic value of (9). When we add the (4) to the (9) it totals to (4). Number (9) is Mars number and it is very indicative of human values. The (4) is the negative number of the Sun. It is the builder's symbol and also very materialistic and negative when coupled with Mars. The influence can be quite undesirable and such was my experience.

In those years, all the casinos had good food and top shows at reasonable prices. There was more than just gambling to lure the patrons. I can still enjoy a visit to Lake Tahoe and Las Vegas.

On one of my more recent visits I had some interesting experiences with the Keno game. One morning at sunrise, I managed to mark a Keno ticket in the upper left-hand section with eight numbers and had six of the numbers light up on the board. I marked the ticket in this manner because three planets were close to the Sun, values (1) and (4), as it rose on that day. This would be similar to the ascendant on an astrological chart of the zodiac. I had missed the big $25,000.00 pay-off but it was nice to see my theory work out.

Another trip to the lake, it was number (3) that was strongly indicated by the astro-aspects. The Sun and the Moon were in the sign ruled by Jupiter, number (3), so, at noon when all these bodies would be at their strongest position, I marked the (3) line both vertical and horizontal for about a half hour before noon and a half hour after noon. The best that I could get was (5) lights on either line. Well, I went to the wash room to clean up for lunch. When I came out I took a look up at the Keno board. There lit up in perfect vertical array was the complete three line that I had been playing. My emotions were mixed to say the least. But, again I had some consolation for my theory.

The next time I made the trip to the casinos was almost a year later. After my experience with the three line, I knew that I would have another chance and hoped to do better. It was the middle of the week when number (5) with (5) planets would be strongly favored. At noon on the (5) day, for a half hour before and after noon, I marked all of the (5) line horizontally and vertically. Twice during that period nine numbers showed up on the same line. Once on the top line and once on the second line. In the astro-numerical descriptions, number (5) is referred to as a dual, neutral number which usually takes on the color of influence of the aspecting bodies or sign that it occupies. In this case line (1) for the Sun and line (2) for the Moon.

One would think that I would be embarrassed to relate these near misses, but, I learned considerable in the process. There is enough evidence in this experience to arrive at some interesting conclusions. As above, so below, does influence punch-outs of the Keno tickets. In astrological terminology, the ascendant area matched the upper left-hand area of the Keno ticket. The mid-heaven area, or, high noon, matched the top of the Keno ticket.

In further consideration of the Keno game, we can note that this name has a total of (4) letters, which is the builders symbol. Perhaps in marking Keno tickets, groups of (4) might prove a certain consistency. The better pay-offs begin with this figure. The phonetic value of Keno adds to (5). This is Mercury's number, also, the (5th) angle is the natural game house of the zodiac. Good directions from Mercury, value (5), as well as from the Sun, values (1) and (4), which rules the (5th) angle of our zodiac, should give the best results. The best percentage pay-off in this game is a double unit of (4) plus (4) equals our famous (8) spot, which pays the limit of $25,000.00, for the least amount invested.

Another factor to keep in mind is that when the day, month and year all coincide, we get a strong figure with which to start. Especially is this true when that particular value, whatever it may be, is well aspected by the Sun and the Moon and other benefics in the zodiac on that particular day. Remember to always add the numbers to a single digit when considering these factors.

We can also note that the best results are usually had when one can eliminate the personal factor. Craps, cards and Roulette all involve personal handling, which opens Pandora's box for complications and abuse. Bingo and Keno are as impersonal as one can get in this gambling area, and, there is less area for abuse.

Roulette is another game somewhat similar to Keno, but, with less pay-out. Roulette has a total of (8) letters. This is Saturn's number which denotes limitation and effort. It has table limits and is not as popular as the other games. It appears more difficult to win when playing the game. The phonetic value of the name Roulette adds to (7). This is the full Moon number. The wheel used in the game is perfectly round and balanced, just as the Sun and Moon appear at the full Moon aspect. This suggests a full cycle of numbers. However, in this game color can be used. Red, Black and Green. Red corresponds to Mars and number (9). Black is Saturn's color symbolized by number (8). Green is related to the Moon and it is symbolized by numbers (2) and (7). An oddity of this game is that there are (2) slots on this wheel that are colored green. Zero and double zero. These have no number value except the phonetic for zero adds to (7). Number (2) is a Moon value, but, being an even number it is colored black. Number (7) is also a Moon number, but, it is colored red. In applying the astro-numerical factors in this game, we associate Mars with the odd numbers and the color red. Saturn is associated with the even numbers and colored black.

As we can see, the Moon's numbers and colors are split. Number (2) is black and Number (7) is red and the Moon's color green falls on the (0) and (00). The house wins and everybody loses when the green slot gets the ball, unless one covers this longshot possibility.

I suppose that the best play in this game would be red and odd numbers when the Sun and Moon are in good strong aspect to Mars, and Jupiter. When the Sun and the Moon are in good strong aspect to Saturn and Venus, then the black and even numbers should be more popular. Green and the zeros I'll leave to the readers discretion.

In the chapter on baseballs and planets, our correlation of the heavens, our zodiac, to the happenings on the baseball diamond and its personnel was very revealing. In this chapter on gambling casinos and Astro-Numerology we can relate in more detail for those interested in the outcome of such events. All games and contests, without exception, are governed by our key phrase; As above, So below.

When the planets, signs and aspects are shown in their numerical values for any particular date, or time, the events on the earth also reflect similar numerical factors. In sporting events the names of the teams and principal participants are of prime consideration. We use the full name description of each team and show the total number of letters added to a single digit.

In baseball games, pitching is of prime importance. When we have totaled the letters in the team's full name description, we then total the letters in the surname of the pitcher for that particular game. The team's numerical value is then added to the numerical value of the pitcher's surname. This total then becomes the key to our interpretation as to which combination fits the Astro aspects for that particular date and time. The combination which matches the total date as well as the individual day value and its aspects the best, is usually the winner.

Following are four games played by the National League baseball teams on Saturday August 20th, 1977, which I have detailed and described for those interested.

First we show the full date and add to a single digit. August is the (8th) month. The 20th adds, (2) plus (0) equals (2). The year adds (1) plus (9) plus (7) plus (7) to (24), or (2) plus (4) equals (6). So, (8) plus (2) plus (6) totals to (16), or, (7). Here we have a (2) day and (7) for the total date. These are Moon value numbers, (2) and (7), so we note the sign the Moon is transiting and the aspects that it is making. We find the Moon in Scorpio, a (9) value and it is parallel and conjoined to Uranus, a (6) value. We can also note that Jupiter, a (3) value is on the cusp of Cancer, which is ruled by the Moon and so we can say that this (3) value is in terms of the (2) and (7) numbers. These are the numbers which we should find in the name values of the winners —, the day value (2), the total date (7), the sign the Moon was transiting, (9) and the (3) and the (6) values.

Our first game shows as follows:

Chicago (5) Los Angeles (4)

Chicago, (7) letters and Cubs (4) letters totals to (11), or, (2) total letters for the team name. Pitching for the Chicago team, which won, was Hernandez (9) letters. When we add the team name total letters, (2), to the pitcher's total surname letters, (9), we total to (11), or, (2). This total net of (2) matches in sign, terms and aspects the key significators of the day and the total date.

The opponents of the Chicago Cubs were the Los Angeles Dodgers. So, we show as follows:

Los Angeles (3) plus (7) letters totals to (10), or, (1). Dodgers (7) letters when added to the (1) total adds to (8) total letters for this team name. Pitching for the Los Angeles team was Rau (3) letters. When we total the (8) plus the (3) we net to (11), or, (2). This (2) value does fit our day and total date values, but, this pitcher was removed in favor of one by the name of Hough, (5) letters. When we total the (5) to the (8) letters for the team name value we total to (13), or (4). This (4) value does not fit the day or total date value and this pitcher was charged with the loss for this game.

Right here it may be of interest to note that on this date Mercury, a (5) value, was slowing down to move into the retrograde motion in relation to our planet earth. In the news on this particular week end it was mentioned that the Dodgers were blowing a big league lead and that the Cincinnati team was closing the gap between them and the Dodgers. In this news item it was mentioned that this pitcher Hough, (5) letters, was not performing as well as he had been. He had all his pitching skills but still when he was used, the team lost. This is a classic example of how Mercury retrograde affects all our activities, and, decisions.

Our second game involved the San Francisco Giants and the Pittsburgh Pirates. So, we show as follows:

San Francisco (5) Pittsburgh (1)

San Francisco (3) plus (9) letters totals to (12), or, (3). Giants (6) letters when added to the (3) total adds to (9) total letters for this team's name. These numbers (3), (6) and the (9) are all factors for the day and the total date. Pitching for the San Francisco team was Halicki (7) letters. When we total the (7) to the (9) total letters for the team's name, we total to (16), or, (1) plus the (6) to (7). This (7) value matches our total date and in turn all the factors for the day value and this team won.

Pittsburgh totals to (10) letters, or (1). Pirates, (7) letters when added to the (1) total nets to an (8) value. Pitching for the Pittsburgh team was Jones (5) letters, which when totaled to the (8) value for the team's name totals to (13), or, (4). This (4) value is not one of our day values, or, factors, and this team lost on this particular day with this pitcher on the mound.

Our third game found the Cincinnati team winning over the New York Mets by a score of (8) to (2). So, we show as follows:

Cincinnati (10), or, (1) total letters, and, Reds (4) letters, total to a (5) for the team's name. Pitching for the Cincinnati team was Moskau (6) letters. When we total the (6) to the team total of (5) we get (11), or, (2). This (2) value matches all our day and total date values and this combination won on this particular day.

New York, (3) plus (4) letters totals to (7). Mets totals to (4) letters. When we add the (7) plus the (4) we total to (11), or, (2). Pitching for the New York team was Espinosa, (8) letters. When we total the (8) to the (2) value we total to (10), or, (1). This (1) value is not one of our day or total date factors and this combination lost on this particular day. It is interesting to note that in this game the score reflects the day value. The most runs that the Mets could generate, (2), on this (2) day, matched the pitcher — team combination of the Reds which added to (2). The total runs that the Reds scored matched the total letters of the losing Met's pitcher, (8).

Our fourth game shows Philadelphia defeating Houston by a score of (5) to (4). So, we note as follows:

Philadelphia (12), or, (3) total letters, and, Phillies (8) letters total to (11), or (2) for the team's name. The Phillies used (2) pitchers to win this game. Christiansen (12), or, (3) letters and Reed, (4) letters. When we total the (3) plus the (4) we get our (7) value. We can note that the (2) for the team and the (7) for the two pitchers both match our day value and our total date value. When we total the pitcher's (7) to the team's number (2) we get a (9) value. This matches the sign that our day value and total date value, (2) & (7), was transiting, that of Scorpio, a (9) value.

Houston, (7) letters, and Astros, (6) letters, total to (13), or, (1) plus the (3) equals (4) for the team name total. Pitching for the Houston club was Niekro, (6) letters. When we total the (6) to the (4) value of the team we get (10), or, (1). This (1) value is not one of our day or total date values and this combination lost on this particular day.

These four games give ample insight as to the proper use of this method of Astro-Cabala for baseball games. Before leaving this method as described, we might also note that the scores, both individual and total, usually match the Day, Total Date, Sign or major aspects shown for that particular time. As in this instance, our other three games totaled to (9) or (6) for their total scores. Chicago won by a score of (5) to (4), which, when added, totals to (9) as does the Philadelphia game which was won by (5) to (4). The San Francisco Giants won by a score of (5) to (1) which adds to our (6) value. The Moon, value (2) & (7), was conjoined to Uranus, a (6) value, on this particular day, in astrological sign of Scorpio, a (9) value.

Football games are quite similar, but, in place of the pitcher, the quarterback, or, star running back, such as an O.J. Simpson, should be considered also when matching the team to the day and total date factors.

Two games that might be of help as examples of our method for the readers more interested in football, follow.

Our first game, that we will detail, was played on August 19th, 1977. The Minnesota Vikings played the Baltimore Colts at Baltimore. This game was played at night on a Friday, which is considered as Venus day with a value of (6). When we add our date, an (8th) month, a (1) day and a (6) year we total to (15), or, (6).

The day value (1) was transiting its own sign. This (1) value represents the Sun and it was transiting Leo, a (1) value, conjoined to Saturn, and (8) value and in aspect to (3), Jupiter and (9), Mars.

The total date (6) was in the Moon's sign Cancer, values (2) and (7), and in aspect to Mercury, a (5) value.

As we can see from the above all our number values from (1) through (9) are all involved in the day and the total date factors. However, the prime number factors are the (1) and the (6), our day value and the total date. So, we note as follows:

Minnesota, (9) letters and Vikings, (7) letters add to (16), or, (1) plus the (6) to a (7) value for the team's name. The quarterback for the Minnesota club was Tarkenton, (9) letters. When we add the (9) to the (7) total letters shown for the team's name, we total to (16), or, (7). This (7) value does not match the day value and Minnesota lost this game.

Baltimore, (9) letters, and Colts, (5) letters, add to a total of (14), or, (1) plus the (4) to a (5) value for the team's name. The quarterback for the Baltimore club was Jones, (5) letters. When we add the (5) total for the team's name to the (5) value of the quarterback we total to (10), or, (1). This matches the day value and Baltimore won this game.

The total date, value (6), showed up in the star running back for the Colts. His name was Ron Lee, (6) letters. He gained (105) yards in this game, which adds (1) plus (0) plus (5) to a total of (6).

An oddity that showed up in this game was reflected in the day value, symbolized by the Sun, values (1) and (4). In the first quarter the winning club scored (10) points, or, (1) plus the (0) equals the (1). In the fourth quarter, the winning club scored (13) points, or (1) plus the (3) equals the (4). Remember that the quarterback and the team's name, the (5) plus the (5) added to (10), or, (1).

The final score was something else to note. Minnesota, (9) letters, and Baltimore, (9) letters ended up with a score of (29) to (7). The (29) plus the (7) adds to (36), which in turn adds (3) plus the (6) to a net of (9).

The above is a very simple approach with only our number values. If and when the individual learns to use the phonetic values and individual phonetic digits, as we do in our chapter in horse racing, much more can be delineated and evaluated. In fact our numbers do become a language in themselves.

The second game selected for an example of our method for football was played on Sunday, August 21st, 1977, between the Los Angeles Rams and the San Francisco Forty Niners.

This date, 8-21-1977, adds (8) plus (3) plus (6) to (17), or, (1) plus the (7) equals (8).

The day value (3), symbolized by Jupiter was transiting Cancer, ruled by the Moon, values (2) nad (7), and was in aspect to the Sun, values (1) and (4) and parallel to Mars, a (9) value.

The total date (8) was symbolized by Saturn, value (8), and this body was conjoined to the Sun in Leo, ruled by the Sun, values (1) and (4), and in aspect to Mars (9) and the Moon, values (2) and (7). So, we note the following:

Los Angeles, (3) plus (7) totals to (10), or, (1). Rams, (4) letters, when added to the (1) value gives us a (5). The Rams used two quarterbacks, Haden (5) letters, and Nameth, (6) letters. When we add the (2) to the team's name value (5), we total to (7). This (7) value does match the day value (3) in terms and the total date by aspect but the factors of the day and total date match their opponents better. So, the San Francisco club won.

San Francisco, (3) plus (9) letters total to (12), or (3). Forty, (5) letters, and Niners, (6) letters totals to (11), or, (2). When we total the (2) value to the (3) value we net to a (5) value. The quarterback for the San Francisco club was Plunkett, (8) letters. When we total the (8) to the (5) name value of the San Francisco club we get (13), or, (4). The conjunction is the strongest aspect in the Astro science and here we find the quarterback, (8) letters, combined with the San Francisco Forty Niners name value (5) adding to the Sun's value (4).

Giving a quick review one can note that San Francisco, (12), or, (3) letters matches the day value and Plunkett, (8) letters, matches our total date value. When the quarterback's (8) value is added to the team's total name value (5), we get (13), or, (4). This (4) value is a Sun value and this game was played on Sunday in San Francisco.

The Los Angeles Rams, (5), and the San Francisco Forty Niners, (5), add to a total of (10), or, (1). The points generated in this game by a score of (23) to (14) total to (37), or, (3) plus the (7) to (10), or, (1). We can also note that each team's total adds to (5). For the San Francisco team, (23), adds (2) plus (3) to (5). For the Los Angeles team, (14), adds (1) plus the (4) to (5).

As we can see from the foregoing, just a simple application of total letters and numbers to the zodiacal planets and sign values can be of tremendous assistance in the selection of winning combinations in the gambling casinos and on the field of play.

This information is not noted here to increase the gambling potential of our readers. It is nothing more than knowledge that has been researched and found to be very consistent. The wisdom of such knowledge will always be in the measure of good that each individual will be able to achieve and apply in his or her own life.

Chapter 11
Astro-Numerology and Horse Racing

The horse racing experience is something apart from the gambling casinos, so, I have allotted a separate chapter for its consideration. Horse racing is considered a sport such as football, baseball and basketball. Down through the years, it has evolved from a meager operation conducted by a few individuals to a giant industry of breeding and performance, requiring legal and professional management. Thousands of jobs are involved and many racing plants operate simultaneously throughout the state, country and world. Unionization has spread through its ranks and the money and taxes generated by this activity aids the revenues of the local, state and federal governments. Charities of all kinds have from time to time benefitted from its operation. Today racing is one of the most popular sports.

The question of gambling in horse racing stems from the ability afforded to individuals to wager on the outcome of any particular race. One can wager to win, place or show. From that simple application the wagering has evolved to an enlargement of its scope to include combinations, daily doubles, exactas and etc; to increase interest and betting totals. Today millions of dollars change hands daily at just one track, so, money is just about the name of the game.

Races are run for prize money. The winner gets the lion's share. The second place horse, or the place horse, receives the next largest share. The show horse, or, the horse that finishes third, receives less than the place horse. In some races for the benefit of the horsemen, there are monies paid right down to the fifth or sixth place horse.

The pari-mutual betting pool represents separate monies wagered by the betting public. These funds are what make the odds that are shown on the totalizator board in the infield at the race track. The totalizator board shows the complete record of money wagered from minute to minute, right up until the time that the race is run. This is the money which is paid to the holders of the win, place or show tickets. The daily double and exacta pools are separate monies and are not reflected on the win, place or show tote board. Tote is a short term for totalizator board.

This tote board is of great interest and importance to the betting public. It tells them much regarding the race. One can tell at a glance who the favorite is, the condition of the track, how many minutes to post time, besides scratches, changes and all the action on all the horses. Besides all this tote board information, there is a daily racing official paper, called the Daily Racing Form. This publication is very complete in news, past performances and present listings for the current day's events. There are also the daily papers with complete listings, — horses, jockeys, weights and probable odds. Everything pertaining to the race fans understanding and handicapping needs are available to them, including an official program and tip sheets.

With all this published data one might think that it should be fairly easy to win money at the race track. A degree of consistency can be achieved, if one is very selective. Disciplining of one's mind and actions at a race track is very difficult. Most folks at the races are out for a good time and to try to make some money. Horse racing is a (5th) angle activity, and, pleasure and speculation are its very essence. Favorites only win about thirty percent of the races. Real longshots win only about five percent of the races. The other sixty five percent are from about three to ten to one in the quoted odds. The (30) percent adds to (3). This is Jupiter's number symbolical of a favorable planetary value or the favorite. The (5) percent is symbolical of the (5th) angle of the zodiac which is speculative and is ruled by the Sun, values (1) and (4) which total to (5). When we take the two words Horse, (5) letters, and Racing, (6) letters they add to (11) or (2). This is the Moon's value and it symbolizes the public and the public's choice. It is the betting public who actually make the odds at the race track. The (65) percent, or (6) plus (5), as we have noted add to (11) or (2). The phonetic values of the (2) words, horse (9) and racing (8), add to (17) or (8). When we note the combination of these (2) planets in astrological practice, we find a tendency to greed. This value (8) also indicates limitation and handicaps. This is the dilemma of horse racing. Greed is the big handicap to conquer to be successful in horse racing. The total letters of horse racing which net to (2) when added to the total phonetic value (8) add to (10) or (1). This is a number (1) sport and is ruled by the Sun, values (1) and (4) which total (5) and rules the (5th) angle of the zodiac.

The words race, (4) letters, and track, (5) letters, add to (9). Again we have Mars' number, and, when formed with the number (5), speculation, and the negative number of the Sun, (4), it builds the speculation into the negative influence of Mars (9). Excess, is one of Mars' negative traits and the race track affords this development, no end. Especially is this noted when we project the phonetic values. Race, (9), and track, (9), which add to (18) or (9). Again we end up with a double Mars value.

The way of participation in this sport of kings, as it is sometimes called, is through the purchase of mutual tickets. One can go to the races and enjoy all the sights and see all the races for a small admission fee. But to participate in the action, one has to purchase a mutual ticket. The words mutual, (6) letters, and ticket, (6) letters add to (12) or (3). These are the money numbers of the zodiac and it takes money to purchase one. No credit cards are acceptable at the mutual windows. Jupiter's number is (3) and it is a growth symbol, (1) plus (2) gives the (3). People who purchase the mutual tickets expect to increase their investment. How much, depends on the odds shown on the tote board. When we consider the phonetic values of the words mutual, (3), and ticket, (3), we find that they total to (6). Again, we have the same money values. So, at the race track, money is the key to the whole operation. Note the word key, (3) letters and a phonetic value of (3) which also totals to our (6), the money number.

All purchases of the mutual tickets are reflected on the tote board in the form of odds and dollars. So, next we shall analyze these four words; odds, dollar and tote board, in our effort to give a reasonable hypothesis as to the nature of this speculative business.

We use the short term of tote, instead of totalizator, because that is the most common term that is used. The words tote, (4) letters, and board, (5) letters, add to (9). This (9) is Mars' number again, indicating a human operation or means devised to conduct the business. It is the symbol of energy, force, or, action that makes the business work. The phonetic value of tote (5) and board (1) add to (6). This is the money number of Venus. When the total letters (9) and the total phonetic (6) are added we still net to our (6). Venus, value (6) rules the second angle of our zodiac, that of money. The energy, or, force is symbolized by money. The amounts in dollars shown on this tote board also reflect the odds.

The word dollar, (6) letters with a phonetic value of (3), when added, totals to (9). This is Mars' number of power, or, force. The dollar, symbolized by the two money numbers (3) and (6), denotes monetary power. The more money put into the mutual pool, the greater the profit to the track and the greater taxes to the government. We use the singular unit in our analysis because the common use in the rate of exchange is known as, the dollar.

The word, odds, (4) letters, is the negative number of the Sun. It is also a builder's symbol of power, the square and the cube. It is powerful in structure. The phonetic value of the word, odds, nets to a (3) value, the money number of growth. The total letters (4) added to the total phonetic (3) gives us a (7) value. This is the full Moon number, symbolical of the full cycle of our numbers (1) through (9).

Here the odds tell the story on the tote board. So many units of tickets times the odds shown on the tote board informs the holder of these tickets, the approximate amount of return, in dollars, if his selection wins that particular race.

The foregoing is a reasonable astro-numerical analysis of just what the horse racing business has to offer the race track patron. Before we get into the selection of probable winners and the amazing consistency of the results, I would like to digress a bit with some personal experience that the author has had at the races.

In the early thirties, right after the 1929 stock market crash, I was working as a bank clerk in Monterey County in California. A friend, with whom I was working, and, a few years my senior, invited me to accompany him to a fair being held at the then exclusive Del Monte Hotel near Monterey. He didn't mention that they were having races, and, that was primarily why he was interested. He financed the whole operation, so, all I had out of the trip was my introduction to horse racing.

It was quite an exclusive crowd and all mingled, rubbing elbows with celebrities, horses, jockeys, trainers and touts. Everything seemed to be so confused. A little old platform with odds posted by hand, no tote boards like we have today. No seating except for a few favored folks. I never saw a race. My friend kept us where he could get what he called, tips, from the right people. Today one would call them touts. He would have to pay them part of his winnings, if they won. The tickets were sold and cashed by hand at small temporary shacks. The thing that surprised me most was that my friend actually won. How the touts found him in the crowd was a mystery to me. I thought of the long hours that I put in at the bank for my small salary and was amazed to see all that money changing hands at the races. This was in the middle of the big depression. Well, it did make its impression on me.

Later, several years later, the economic picture did improve, and, with the financial improvement, I found that I had to work less, made more money and had more time for other things. Somewhere after World War Two, I stumbled across a book on numerology and astrology that impressed me very much. So much so, that I actually learned to cast a horoscope, and, learned to read it. I used to cast charts for all my friends. I was never influenced by money, I did it all for my own experience. I amazed myself with the results that I achieved. I became even more interested. I subscribed to magazines and accumulated an astrological library.

My experience at the races in Del Monte stuck with me, and, between all my other research and reading I used my Saturdays to test the astro-aspects and my newly created English cabala at the race track. Each race, usually in less than two minutes time, gave me instant proof as to my ability. It has only been in recent years that I managed to achieve real consistency. In the process, I have had a few interesting experiences which I think might be of interest and value to the readers.

I will start with an early episode at a San Francisco Bay Area track. It was a feature race, I believe a $50,000.00 handicap race. Calumet Farms had an odds on, (3) to (5) favorite, in the race. I believe the horse's name was A. Gleam. A local restaurant man had an (80) to (1) longshot in the race. Another horse, whose name also escapes me, but, I remember that the odds were (12) to (1). All seemed to look like runners when I applied the Astro-aspects to the name and post position. So, inexperienced as I was, instead of wagering the way I would do today, bet the two longest prices to place; I bought a win ticket on the (3) to (5) favorite. Then I bet the two long prices to show. Well, the horses finished one, two, three. But, not the finish that I had handicapped. In the middle of the stretch run, the favorite, A Gleam, was galloping down the stretch three lengths in front, when the jockey on this horse, Euclid le Blanc, stood up in the stirrups and steadied the horse. At this point the other two longshots roared past. The (80) to (1) price won, the (12) to (1) finished second and the favorite, A. Gleam, finished third. There I sat holding three tickets with a total value of $8.00. Sure, I won $2.00 on the race, but, that was little consolation. Today I would never bet to win only, and, never on a (3) to (5) favorite. If I had that race to play again, it would be on the two price horses to place. The reason for this you will understand when I relate my next experience. Incidently, Calumet Farms racing silks, were never seen in Northern California again, and, jockey, Euclid le Blanc, just gradually faded from the racing scene.

On the last day of a season of racing at Bay Meadows, I stayed to bet on a horse in the last race. I forgot the year and the name of the horse, but, never the experience. I was at the finish line of this particular race and had a clear view. In this race my horse was about (5) to (1). I had learned my lesson well, for this time I was betting to place. There I was right at the finish and some other horse beat my selection by a good neck. A photo sign went up on the board, but, I didn't mind as my horse finished second and that is the way that I bet it. Off I went to the cashier's window. Before I could get there, my horse was shown as the winner. Well, I cashed my ticket and headed to the place where the photo would be posted. I waited and waited but no photo was posted.

When I arrived home, I thought about it and realized that something wasn't kosher. So, I wrote to the Commissioner of Horse Racing for the State of California. I was informed that a formal investigation would be made.

A couple of weeks later I was invited back to the Bay Meadows race track at a spring meet as a guest of the management and they gave me the red-carpet treatment. They took me on a personal tour of the photo system at the track. I was told that there was no photo posted for the last race of the last meet. I was also told that the chap responsible for the oversight was fired, but, was reinstated by his union.

I then realized the power and influence of labor unions at the race track. I have often had to stand and wait until mutual clerks, working at the sellers windows, got all their tickets punched out first before they would start punching customer's tickets. I also remember a strike for an outrageous increase in wages at one track. After half of the racing days were gone down the drain, tying up funds, jobs, and costing the State dearly in taxes lost, the Union boss finally had to tell the clerks to get back to work and accept the increase that management had suggested.

Strangely all these incidents haven't dampened the interest in the sport. If anything, the crowds are bigger than ever.

One of the most questionable races to win is the Kentucky Derby. A lot of owners pay fees and enter their horses just to say that they had a horse run in the derby. Others who have good colts don't even bother to enter. This is a prestige race, in that the winners of it command high stud fees for breeding purposes. It is also the first leg of the triple crown. Very few horses ever win all three races of the triple crown, which consists of the Derby, Preakness and the Belmont Stakes. This is particularly so with horses from California. The change in climate and water alone needs time for adjustment.

Horses are like people in this respect, although I believe that certain horses are smarter than people. I wonder how many of the readers have ever heard of Lady Wonder. This horse was a grey mare owned by a lady near Washington, D.C. They found out that this horse was psychic. They even built a large typewriter for her. Anyone could ask a question by writing it down on a piece of paper and the owner would read it to the mare. Then the mare would spell out the answer by knocking the letters of her typewriter down to a hanging position to spell out the answer. She was accurate up to about (80) percent of the time. Even congressmen came to question the amazing mare. Astounding as this may be, I also read where some German horses were taught how to do square-root.

I once read about a California trainer who not only brought water all the way from California, but, food as well, just to make sure that his horse could adjust properly to his new environment. This trainer even slept with his horse. He must have known just what he had to do because his horse went on to win the Kentucky Derby.

The derby is a very rough race. Bumping and jockeying for position can eliminate a horse early. Very few claims of foul have been allowed. This is quite a contrast to other race tracks where stewards have disqualified horses for just very slight infractions. Perhaps this is because everybody around a race track wagers on the races. Who are in a better position to protect their wagers?

There is a certain amount of hypocrisy around the race track. They like to make things look honest and true. I knew a trainer who once told me that he conditioned his horses in the races. Only he knew when his horse was ready, and, even when he was ready, he would wait until he found the right spot to turn him loose. This was valuable information that he could sell to the touts, who are not allowed around the race track. This kind of operation would tend to explain the large odds on daily doubles and exactas and etc.

In the San Francisco Bay Area one owner was drinking in the track's bar and casually mentioned that he and his trainer didn't always try to win every race. The track's officials barred him from the track for a whole year. This seems to be a regular practice though nobody will admit it openly or they will be censured.

The stewards at the track are supposed to protect the betting public by disqualifying any unfit horse. Such as lame horses, doped horses or any horse that is injured on the way to post. Horses that break away from the outriders and run away around the track and use up their speed, are also scratched by the stewards. But I have seen horses that seemed unfit allowed to go to post. One such case was a race for colts and fillies at a spring meet. This colt in the parade to post was following a filly and had a two foot erection. Considerable money was wagered on this animal but he was not scratched. He ran like his mind was on anything but racing.

No matter how honest the rules try to keep the business, we still are coping with the human problem. Of course in the process of racing there are spills, horses shy at objects and equipment fails. All this tends to afford truth to the saying that; there is no sure thing in racing.

Notwithstanding all this, the astro-numerical application does pin-point runners that usually win or run second. The readers can judge for themselves from the charts that I have included in the next chapter, 11-A.

Chapter 11-A
The Chart and the
Complete Racing Card
Astro-Numerological Race Selections

In January, 1977, I made a special trip to Santa Anita race track to be at the races when Mercury was direct, the weather fair and the track not too crowded. This turned out to be Wednesday, Thursday and Friday, the 26th, 27th and 28th. For inclusion in this chapter, I have selected the chart that I erected for the 26th together with the full listings and the two horses that finished first and second, in each race. I shall also recap the race factors to show how the selections were made.

Races are usually run in the afternoon hours, so, the chart in this book covers the zodiac and aspects between the hours of noon to 6 P.M. Also, only the degree of the mid-heaven and the ascendant are listed for each half hour. These are the most important points when matching the program entries to the zodiac. The mid-heaven, or, M.C. as it is referred to by most astrologers, is the most preferential point. On the program, the horse's number and post position are usually the same and this factor is usually reflected in the M.C. or ascendant value or aspects to this degree. The M.C., degree and aspects usually are also reflected in the number of letters and phonetic values in all the names associated with the entry. Such as, the name of the horse, jockey and the trainer.

In our application of our number references, we use numbers (1) and (4) to indicate similar values of the Sun. Also (2) and (7) to indicate similar values of the Moon. So in our chart we show only numbers (1) and (2) and omit numbers (4) and (7). In this application (1) and (4) are considered as similar values. This is also how we use the (2) and the (7). They are interchangeable or both indicative of the same value.

In the phonetics we use only the initial digits. These are the numerical values of the first sound of a name. This affords speed in our aspect reference. In our astro-numerical cabala, both the initial digits and the full phonetic value of a name give remarkable clues to the character and abilities of man or animal.

When I arrive at the track, I purchase a program and pin my chart to the inside of the cover of the program for easy reference. I get a reserved seat and sit down, and, go to work. I usually arrive about an hour before the first post time, so that I can write as much information as I can on my program. This information includes the total letters of each entry and all the initial digits. The names of the horses can be in single, double or triple parts. Above each part I show the total letters. To the right of the last part of the name I show the grand total of the name's letters. When the entry has only one name, or, one word to the name, the lone total of the letters is shown to the right of the name.

I only use the last surname of the trainer or jockey when showing the I.D.'s, or, initial digits. The I.D. of each horse is the initial sound of each word in the name of the horse. We show this factor under the first letter of each word in the horses name. If there is more than one word in the name of the horse, we add the I.D.'s and show the total under the number on the program shown for that horse.

In considering each race, we treat it as representing that particular numbered house, or, angle of the zodiac of the heavens. Remember; As above, so below! The first race is also symbolized by the Sun, number (1) and (4) values, so, we first note the Sun's present sign by transit and its aspects. We write these at the top of the page in a convenient spot. We also show the sign and degree of the M.C. and the ascendant plus the prime aspects for the post time shown on the tote board for that particular race. After a little practice, all this can be done for each race in about five or ten minutes. To this information we also note the number of post position and make sure that each horse is running out of that numbered post position. If the post position differs from the number listed for that horse we also note his post position to the left of that horse's number.

When the post time shown is other than the hour, or half hour, we estimate the approximate off time for the M.C. and ascendant factors. In this application just approximate calculations work just fine.

Following is the chart erected for January 26th, 1977.

Chart For January 26th, 1977

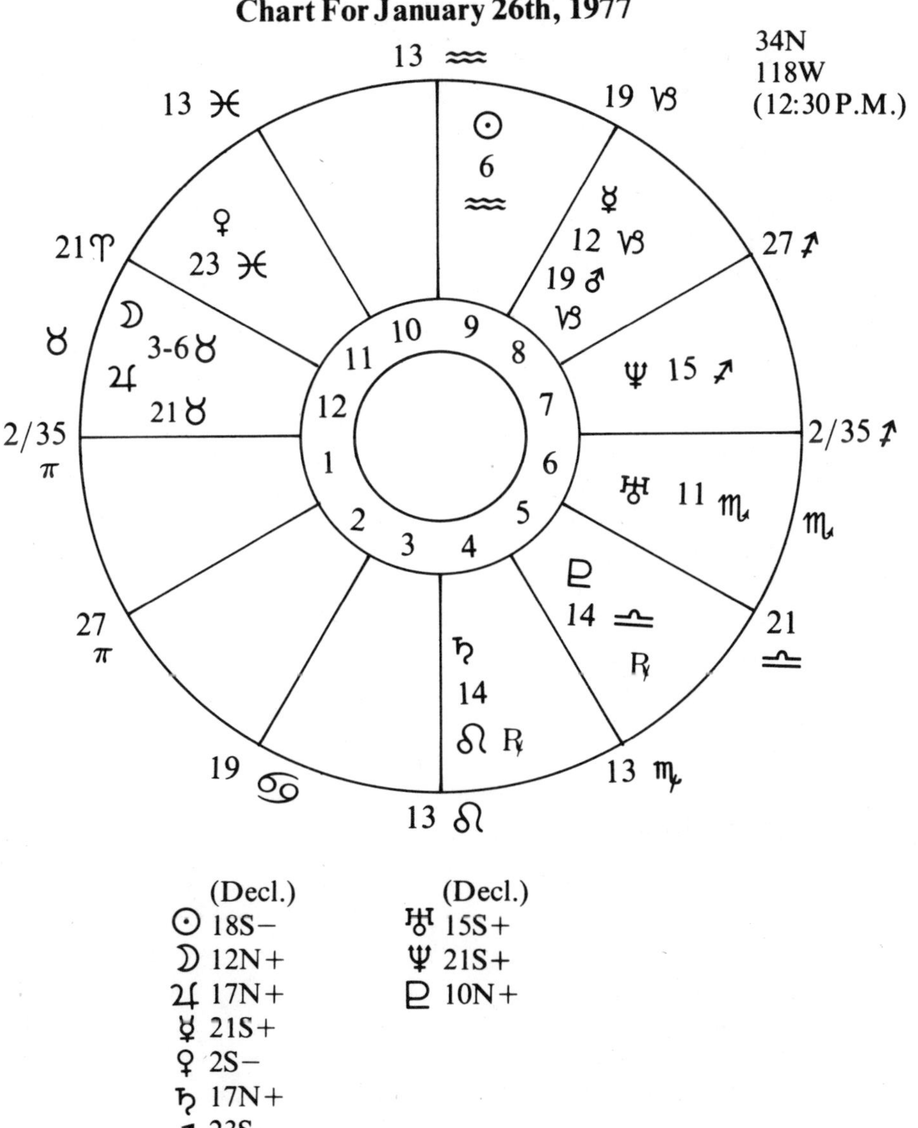

(Decl.)
⊙ 18S−
☽ 12N+
♃ 17N+
☿ 21S+
♀ 2S−
♄ 17N+
♂ 23S−

(Decl.)
♅ 15S+
Ψ 21S+
♇ 10N+

89

Ephemeris readings for M.C. and ascendant on January 26th, 1977 for each half hour from noon to 5:30 P.M. at latitude 34 north and longitude 118 west.

Pacific Standard Time	Siderial Time	M.C.	Ascendant
12:00 (Noon)	20:31	5 Aquarius	23 Taurus
12:30 P.M.	21:01	13 Aquarius	3 Gemini
1:00 P.M.	21:31	20 Aquarius	10 Gemini
1:30 P.M.	22:01	28 Aquarius	18 Gemini
2:00 P.M.	22:31	6 Pisces	25 Gemini
2:30 P.M.	23:01	14 Pisces	2 Cancer
3:00 P.M.	23:31	22 Pisces	9 Cancer
3:30 P.M.	0:01	0 Aries	17 Cancer
4:00 P.M.	0:31	9 Aries	22 Cancer
4:30 P.M.	1:01	17 Aries	28 Cancer
5:00 P.M.	1:31	25 Aries	2 Leo
5:30 P.M.	2:01	3 Taurus	11 Leo

Aspects

Number	Planetary Body	Terms	Number Value
(1) and (4)	Sun	Aquarius	8

Aspects applying or within orb	Number Value
Parallel and opposed to Saturn	8
Square to the Moon	2 and 7
Parallel to Jupiter	3
Square to Uranus	6
Semi-square to Venus	6
Semi-sextile to Mercury	5
Closest planet to the Sun is Mars	9

Other Notes:
Saturn, value (8) is also in mutual reception with the Sun and gains in power by this aspect.

Number	Planetary Body	Terms	Number Value
(2) and (7)	Moon	Taurus	6

Aspects applying or within orb	Number Value
Square to the Sun	1 and 4
Opposed to Uranus	6
Applying to square of Saturn	8
Applying to a conjunction of Jupiter	3
Applying to a trine of Mercury	5

Number	Planetary Body	Terms	Number Value
(3)	Jupiter	Taurus	6

Aspects applying or within orb	Number Value
Sextile to Venus (Mutual Reception)	6
Applying to a conjunction of the Moon	2 and 7
Trine to Mars	9
Parallel to the Sun	1 and 4
Parallel to Saturn	8
Applying to a trine of Mercury	5

Number	Planetary Body	Terms	Number Value
(5)	Mercury	Capricorn	8
	Neptune	Sagittarius	3

Aspects applying or within orb	Number Value
Mercury conjoined and parallel Mars	9
Applying trine to the Moon	2 and 7
Separating semi-sextile the Sun	1 and 4
Applying trine to Jupiter	3
Applying sextile to Venus	6
Sextile Uranus	6
Quincunx Saturn	8
Square to Pluto	9
Neptune is Sextile to Pluto	9
Neptune is Trine to Saturn	8
Neptune is Semi-sextile Mars	9
Neptune is Semi-sextile Uranus	6

Number	Planetary Body	Terms	Number Value
(6)	Venus	Pisces	3
	Uranus	Scorpio	9

Aspects applying or within orb	Number Value
Venus is trine to Jupiter	3
Sextile to Mars	9
Applying semi-square to the Sun	1 and 4
Friendly terms (Moon in Taurus)	2 and 7
Uranus is Sextile to Mercury	5
Square to Saturn	8
Square to the Sun	1 and 4
Applying to opposition of Moon	2 and 7

Venus in Pisces and Jupiter in Taurus
are in strong mutual reception aspect
to each other.

Number	Planetary Body	Terms	Number Value
(8)	Saturn	Leo	1 and 4

Aspects applying or within orb	Number Value
Applying parallel and opposed to Sun in strong mutual reception	1 and 4
Parallel to Jupiter	3
Applying square to the Moon	2 and 7
Square to Uranus	6
Trine to Neptune	5
Sextile to Pluto	9

Other Notes:
(Mars and Mercury in terms of Saturn)

Number	Planetary Body	Terms	Number Value
(9)	Mars	Capricorn	8
	Pluto	Libra	6

Aspects applying or within orb	Number Value
Mars in sextile aspect to Venus	6
Mars trine aspect to Jupiter	3
Mars conjoined to Mercury	5
Mars semi-sextile to Neptune	5
Mars quincunx to Saturn	8
Mars is the closest planet to the Sun	1 and 4
Pluto is sextile to Saturn	8
Semi-sextile to Uranus	6
Sextile to Neptune	5
Square to Mercury	5

The foregoing detailed descriptions of the mutual aspects
between the planets of the chart can be noted in much less space
by using our astrological symbols and numbers which the
author has found more convenient. Following is a sample work
sheet.

ZODIACAL CHART

For Latitude	Longitude	Date: January 26th, 1977
34 north	118 west	

Pacific Std. Time		Sidereal Time	M.C.	Asc.
12:00	Noon	20:31	5 Aquarius	23 Taurus
12:30		21:01	13 Aquarius	3 Gemini
1:00		21:31	20 Aquarius	10 Gemini
1:30		22:01	28 Aquarius	18 Gemini
2:00		22:31	6 Pisces	25 Gemini
2:30		23:01	14 Pisces	2 Cancer
3:00		23:31	22 Pisces	9 Cancer
3:30		:01	0 Aries	17 Cancer
4:00		:31	9 Aries	22 Cancer
4:30		1:01	17 Aries	28 Cancer
5:00		1:31	25 Aries	5 Leo
5:30		2:01	3 Taurus	11 Leo

Semi-Square

(1)	L	21 (Pisces & Sagittarius)
(2)	L	18-21 (Gemini & Pisces)
(3)	L	6 (Cancer & Aries)
(5)	L	27 (Aquarius & Scorpio)
(6)	L	8 (Taurus & Aquarius)
(8)	L	29 (Virgo & Gemini)
(9)	L	4 (Pisces & Sagittarius)

Other

Uranus (6)	11 Scorpio
Neptune (5)	15 Sagittarius
Pluto (9)	14 Libra

(continued)

Zodiacal Chart Continued

Decl.:	18S−	12N+	17N+	21S+	2S−	17N+	23S−
	Sun	Moon	Jupiter	Mercury	Venus	Saturn	Mars
	(1)	(2)	(3)	(5)	(6)	(8)	(9)
Deg.:	6	3/6	21	12	23	14	19
Sign:	Aquarius	Taurus	Taurus	Capricorn	Pisces	Leo	Capricorn

Sun in	Moon in	Jupiter	Mercury	Venus	Saturn	Mars
(8)	(6)	in (6)	in (8)	in (3)	in (1)	in (8)
in	in	in	in	in	in	in
aspect	aspect	aspect	aspect	aspect	aspect	aspect
to (5)	to (1)	to (6)	to (2)	to (3)	to (3)	to (5)
(2)	(8)	(9)	(6)	(9)	(5)	(6)
(6)	(6)	(8)	(9)	(1)	(6)	(3)
(3)	(3)	(2)	(1)	(2)	(9)	
and	(5)	(1)		Moon	Sun	
Saturn		Venus		in (6)	in (8)	
in Leo		in		Jupiter	Mercury	
(1)		Pisces		in (6)	in (8)	
		(3)			Mars	
					in (8)	

January 26th, 1977
First Race   Santa Anita

Number	Name		Trainer	Jockey	Morn. Line odds
		(Total Letters)			
		5 1			
(1)	CINDY Q		(6) Blincoe	Sellers	15
		6 2	2	6	
Total		7 4			
(4) (2)	GENUINE LADY		(2) Palma	Pincay	3
ID6		3 3	8	8	
		5 4			
(3)	ROYAL LORE		(9) Penny	Diaz	30
		2 3	8	4	
		1 4 2 4			
(4)	A KISS OF WIND		(2) Stute	Centeno	4
		1 2 2 6	6	6	
		8 4			
(5)	CONTRARY LADY		(3) Priddy	Campas	8
		2 3	8	2	
(6)	QUIVET		(6) Euster	Vargas	12
		2	1	6	
		5 1 5			
(7)	RAISE A SCENE		(2) Rettele	Skinner	6
		2 1 6	2	6	
Total		8 6			
(4) (8)	DOUBTFUL DEBBIE		(5) Shima	Noguez	15
ID8		4 4	3	5	
		9 6			
(9)	DECORATOR DANCER		(6) Glauberg	Toro	10
		4 4	2	4	
(10)	JENAKA		(6) Doyle	McHargue	5
		3	4	4	
		6 4			
(11)	SAVAGE CALL		(1) Hine	Pineda	30
		6 2	8	8	
		7 6			
(12)	MANILLA SQUARE		(4) Cofer	Olivares	20
		4 6	2	2	

In consideration of the first race we note that the post time shown on the tote board was the same as listed on the program, 12:30 P.M. This then validates the time for which our chart is erected. So, we note as follows:

	Number Value
M.C. 13 degrees of Aquarius	(8)
Asc. 3 degrees of Gemini	(5)
Aspects	**Number Value**
Sun trine the ascendant	(1) and (4)
Moon semi-sextile ascendant	(2) and (7)
Uranus square the M.C.	(6)
Saturn opposed the M.C.	(8)
Neptune sextile the M.C.	(5)
Pluto trine the M.C.	(9)

At the time this race was run we find that Saturn (8) and Neptune (5) are angular by position. So, besides looking for the Sun's prime aspects as the prime significator of the first race, we must acknowledge the power of the angular bodies. In this case, Saturn (8) and Neptune (5).

In looking at our figures shown for the horses listed in the first race, we find that the morning line favorite shows all the race factors in its number, I.D., total letters and in the I.D.'s of the jockey and trainer. This entry became a strong selection. In reviewing the other selections, the number (8) horse with a total letters of (5) caught my eye. This horse was listed at (15) to (1) in the morning line odds.

Of course our M.C. showed a value of (8) and the ascendant a value of (5). These two values are also symbolized by Saturn (8) and Neptune (5) which were strong by angular position at the time this race was to be run. The first race, symbolized by the Sun, (1) and (4) values, was in strong mutual reception aspect with Saturn (8). As the Sun was in square orb to the Moon, and the favorite was in the (2) post position, I had doubts about its winning this race. Upon checking further we can note that I.D. of the number (2) horse totaled to a (6) value. Though this body Venus (6) was elevated and rising it was applying to a semi-square aspect to our prime race factor, the

Sun. Also Uranus (6) was in square aspect to the Sun. The number (8) horse had a unit-force I.D. of (4) plus (4) which totaled to (8). Saturn (8) was located on the cusp of the (4th) angle of our chart in powerful mutual reception aspect to our prime race factor, the Sun. As the (4th) cusp Leo was ruled by the Sun and this angle signifies the end of the matter in horary astrology, I judged that this number (8) horse would be the winner.

As I am an ultra-conservative with any gambling action, I decided to wager both these horses, the number (8) and the number (2) to place. Well, the number (8) horse won, wire to wire, and the number (2) finished second. This was a good beginning for this particular outing.

January 26th, 1977
Second Race   Santa Anita

Number	Name		Trainer	Jockey	Morn. Line odds
	5 9	(Total Letters)			
(1)	FLEET BUCKMAKER	(5)	McBride	Lambert	5
	8 2		4	3	
	7 8				
(2)	GETAWAY TERRESTO	(6)	Cambell	Sellers	6
	2 4		2	6	
	5 3 5				
(3)	FLEET AND READY	(4)	Boehner	Noquez	15
	8 1 2		2	5	
	4 4				
(4)	OBIE TUFF	(8)	Pollard	Gonzales	30
	6 4		8	2	
(5)	SASABE	(6)	Cleveland	Diaz	20
	6		2	4	
	3 5				
(6)	SIR HONOR	(8)	West	Howard	8
	6 2		6	8	
Total	3 8				
(9) (7)	FLY AMERICAN	(2)	Frankel	Pincay	8/5
ID9	8 1		8	8	
Total	5 6				
(1) (8)	REGAL INTENT	(2)	King	Mercado	12
ID3	2 1		2	4	
	6 4				
(9)	RULLAH FOLS	(1)	Bernstein	Gampas	4
	2 8		2	2	
	8 4				
(10)	THIRTEEN PLUS	(3)	Manzi	Munoz	20
	9 8		4	4	

During January and February in 1977 at Santa Anita the races were run during the afternoon at about half hour intervals. So, at 1:00 P.M. for the second race we note the following:

	Number Value
M.C. 20 degrees of Aquarius	(8)
Asc. 10 degrees of Gemini	(5)

Aspects	Number Value
Jupiter square the M.C.	(3)
Mars semi-sextile M.C.	(9)
Venus semi-sextile M.C.	(6)
Saturn applying sextile Asc.	(8)
Pluto applying sextile Asc.	(9)

Our prime race factors become the (2) and (7), this being the second race symbolical of the Moon, values (2) and (7). The Moon was in the same sign as Jupiter so we consider the Moon as applying to a conjunction of Jupiter our prime M.C. aspecting body. These two planets are in Taurus ruled by Venus in terms of value (6). Taurus is the natural (2nd) angle of our zodiac and rules amongst other things, money. Jupiter in astrological terms is considered benefic. So, in conjunction with the Moon, would indicate a popular public choice. In racing jargon this would be the favorite.

In the number (7) horse in this (2nd) race we find a total of (2) for the letters. These numbers not only match the prime race factors, but this horse was the morning line favorite listed at odds of (8) to (5). The odds reflect our M.C. and Asc. factors, shown for the post time for this race. This number (7) horse becomes our prime selection to win this race. The I.D.'s for the horse's name, the trainer and the jockey also fit our prime race factors by aspects to the M.C. and ascendant at the time this race was run. The I.D.'s add, horse (9) plus trainer (8) plus Jockey (8) to (25) or a net of (7).

Immediately adjacent to the number (7) horse in post position (8) we find another selection with a net of (2) for the total letters in the name of the horse. This selection totaled to an I.D. of (3). The trainer showed an I.D. of (2). The jockey's

I.D. was (4). These are all prime race factors. This selection was listed at (12) to (1) in the morning line so I picked this horse to finish second.

The favorite won the race rather easily and the number (8) finished second and paid more than the winner.

When we project the second house cusp of (27) degrees of Gemini to the ascendant we find that (13) degrees of Virgo falls on the cusp of the fourth. Mercury then becomes the ruler of both the ascendant and the (4th) angle cusp. Mercury is posited in terms of Saturn conjoined to Mars (9). Pluto (9) is also in this (4th) angle by this projection. When we check our selections we find that the winner, number (7) plus the (2) for the letters add to (9). Also the winning horse had an I.D. of (9). The horse that ran second showed an I.D. of (3) plus the I.D. for the trainer (2) plus an I.D. for the jockey (4) that adds to (9). Our numbers do become a language in themselves.

<h1 style="text-align:center">January 26th, 1977</h1>
<h2 style="text-align:center">Third Race   Santa Anita</h2>

Number	Name	(Total Letters)	Trainer	Jockey	Morn. Line odds
(1)	COUNTRY FEVER 7 5 2 8	(3)	Robbins 2	Pincay 8	4
Total (6) (2) ID4	KID KONFIDENCE 3 1 2 2	(4)	King 2	Mercado 4	12
Total (2) (3) ID9	ALE HOUSE 3 5 1 8	(8)	Mulhall 4	Shoemaker 3	8
(4)	CONCUSSION 2	(1)	Potter 8	McHargue 4	6
(5)	SKARA BRAE 5 4 6 2	(9)	Canty 2	Casteneda 2	7/2
(6)	LITHOTOMIST 3	(2)	Mandella 4	Gonzalez 2	20
(7)	HENOSEE 8	(7)	Darfman 4	Valenzuela 6	30
(8)	HENNEPIN COUNTY 8 6 8 2	(5)	Martin 4	Campas 2	20
(9)	REFICAN 2	(7)	Mayer 4	DiNicola 4	20
Total (3) (10) ID3	ABE THE GREAT 3 3 5 1 9 2	(2)	Blincoe 2	Sellers 6	3
(11)	SWOT 6	(4)	Stute 6	Centeno 6	20
(12)	SOLDIER 6	(7)	Whittingham 6	Mena 4	30

101

For the (3rd) race we note the following:

	Number Value
M.C. 28 degrees of Aquarius	(8)
Asc. 18 degrees of Gemini	(5)

Aspects	**Number Value**
Moon applying sextile the M.C.	(2) and (7)
Mercury separating semi-square M.C.	(5)
Venus rising in the (10th) angle	(6)
Moon semi-square ascendant	(2) and (7)
Neptune separating opposition the asc.	(5)
Jupiter semi-sextile the ascendant	(3)

Our prime race factor (3) is symbolized by Jupiter (3) which we find conjoined to the Moon (2) and (7) values in terms Venus (6) which rules Taurus. Venus (6), our most elevated body for the time of the running of this race, is in its exalted terms in mutual reception and sextile aspect to our prime race factor, Jupiter (3). The Moon and Jupiter are also rising and elevated. Jupiter is also in parallel aspect to the Sun, values (1) and (4), and trine to Mars (9).

When we project the (19) degrees of Cancer which falls on the (3rd) cusp of our chart to the ascendant point, we find that the (4th) cusp shows (21) degrees of Libra and Venus (6) becomes the ruler of the end of the matter in question. We also find that Uranus (6) falls within the confines of this angle. The race ruler Jupiter (3) conjoined to the projected ascendant ruler Moon in terms of Venus the (4th) ruler of the end of the matter and all three of these bodies elevated and strong by aspect, I was led to the top of the list of the horses in this race. The number (2) horse with a total of (4) for the letters added to our (6) value. In our projected position the Sun, values (1) and (4) became angular in the (7th) house and this body is making the closest aspect to our most elevated body, the Moon (2) and (7) in this projection. This number (2) horse showed a (2) plus (2) which totaled to (4) for its I.D. The trainer showed a (2) for his I.D. and the jockey showed a (4). When we add the I.D.'s for the horse Jockey and trainer we total to (10) or (1). This horse at (12) to (1) in the line odds looked real good. My second selection became the favorite at (3) to (1) in the morning line odds. This horse had number (10) post, which, when added to his total for the letters (2), netted to (3), our prime race factor. It also had an I.D. of (3). The trainer showed an I.D. of (2) and the jockey showed an I.D. of (6).

When the race was over the number (2) horse had won and the number (10) finished second.

January 26th, 1977
Fourth Race

Santa Anita

Number	Name	(Total Letters)	Trainer	Jockey	Morn. Line odds
		8 7			
(1)	CHIPPEWA CHARLIE	(6)	Threewitt	Diaz	15
		8 8	9	4	
Total		3 3			
(8) (2)	THE FOP	(6)	Rose	Toro	7/5
ID8		9 8	2	4	
		3 5			
(3)	HAZ HOLME	(8)	Blimcoe	Olivares	30
		8 8	2	2	
		5 6			
(4)	BAKER STREET	(2)	Whittingham	Martini	50
		2 6	6	4	
		4 4 1			
(5)	JOSE KANU C	(9)	King	Mercado	10
		8 2 6	2	4	
		5 4			
(6)	BALLY HOOP	(9)	Nickerson	Castaneda	12
		2 8	5	2	
		6 5			
(7)	SAVAGE DANCE	(2)	Martin	Campas	20
		6 4	4	2	
Total		4 6			
(9) (8)	SURE DOUBLE	(1)	Campbell	Lambert	2
ID7		3 4	2	3	
		3 6			
(9)	OLD FRIEND	(9)	Whittingham	Shoemaker	12
		6 8	6	3	
(10)	SUMMIT	(6)	Parker	Sellers	15
		6	8	6	
		8 4			
(11)	STARTING TIME	(3)	Stucki	Skinner	30
		6 4	6	6	
		3 7			
(12)	ALI FRAZIER	(1)	Glauburg	Pierce	30
		1 8	2	8	

The time listed for the running of the (4th) race showed the following degrees on the angles.

	Number Value
M.C. 6 degrees of Pisces	(3)
Asc. 25 degrees of Gemini	(5)

Aspects	**Number Value**
Sun semi-sextile M.C.	(1) and (4)
Moon sextile M.C.	(2) and (7)
Venus rising in the (10th)	(6)
Saturn applying semi-square the Asc.	(8)

The above angle points again show the Moon, Jupiter and Venus rising and elevated. The number (2) horse listed in the morning line at (7) to (5) was the solid favorite. This being the (4th) race our prime race factor becomes the Sun, values (1) and (4). Leo falls on the (4th) cusp of this chart and Saturn (8) is almost exactly conjoined to this point. Saturn is our planetary symbol of form, in our racing interpretations. When we move our (13) degrees of Leo, which is found on the cusp of the (4th) angle, to the ascendant point, Sagittarius falls on the cusp of the (4th) angle. This sign ruled by Jupiter, a (3) value, indicates that in the end our number (2) horse, (Moon conjoined to Jupiter) should prevail. Jupiter is also parallel to the Sun, our prime race factor. The number (2) horse shows a unit-force of (3) plus (3) to a total of (6) for its letters. This Venus value (6) is our most elevated planetary value at the time this race was run and it is in mutual reception sextile aspect to Jupiter (3) which rules the end of the matter, or race. The I.D. of the horse totaled to our Saturn value (8). The number (2) post plus the total letters (6) also add to our Saturn value (8). This Saturn value is in strong mutual reception aspect to our prime race value the Sun. The ID's of the horse (8) plus the trainer (2) plus the jockey (4) total to (14) or (5). This (5) value is symbolical of our Neptune (5) which is found in the angular position in both our original and projected charts.

This race, having such strong indications of a formful performance, focused attention on the second choice in the morning line at (2) to (1) to finish second. This horse showed number (8) for the post and a total of (1) for the letters. The I.D.'s of the horse, trainer and jockey not only fit the prime race factors but they also totaled to (3) the ruler of the projected (4th) angle cusp and mutual reception factor of our most elevated planet, Venus.

The number (2) won and the number (8) ran second for an easy bit of handicapping.

January 26th, 1977
Fifth Race   **Santa Anita**

Number	Name	(Total Letters)	Trainer	Jockey	Morn. Line odds
		5 4			
(1)	ZULLA ROAD	(9)	Moreno	Campas	30
		7 2		4	2
(2)	SCHON	(5)	Jordan	Meno	6
		3		3	4
		4 4			
(3)	SING BACK	(8)	Jones	Toro	3
		6 2		3	4
		2 6			
(4)	MS NUDINI	(8)	Rettele	Shoemaker	5
		4 5		2	3
Total		6 5			
(7) (5)	NASHUA TRYST	(2)	Hronec	Sellers	12
ID9	5 4			2	6
		3 4			
(6)	ALA ANNA	(7)	Tinsley	Mercado	30
		1 1		4	4
		6 6			
(7)	HONEY'S POLICY	(3)	Mandella	Castaneda	10
		8 8		4	2
(8)	SADRULLAH	(9)	Coffee	Gonzales	12
		6		2	2
Total		1 4			
(5) (9)	THIRTEENTH HOPE	(5)	Vienna	DiNicola	12
ID8	9 8			6	4
		2 8			
(10)	LA VENCEDOR	(1)	Frankel	Pincay	4
		3 6		8	8
		6 4			
(11)	MUNDEN MISS	(1)	Euster	McHargue	12
		4 4		1	4
		4 3 5			
(12)	LETS GET LUCKY	(3)	Potter	Howard	15
		3 2 3		8	8

107

Post time for the (5th) race found the following degrees on the cusp of our angles.

	Number Value
M.C. 14 degrees Pisces value	(3)
Asc. 2 degrees Cancer value	(2) and (7)
Aspects	**Number Value**
Mercury sextile M.C.	(5)
Mars sextile M.C.	(9)
Uranus trine M.C.	(6)
Neptune square M.C.	(5)
Pluto quincunx M.C.	(9)
Venus in the (10th) angle rising	(6)
Moon sextile the Asc.	(2) and (7)
Sun quincunx the Asc.	(1) and (4)

This being the (5th) race and Mercury (5) ruling the cusp of our (5th) angle of the chart focuses attention on this (5) value. We find that Mercury (5) falls in the fourth angle when we progress our (5th) angle cusp to the ascendant position. Sagittarius falls on the cusp of the (4th) angle in this position. Jupiter (3) was in trine aspect to Mars (9) which also falls in the fourth angle conjoined to Mercury (5). Jupiter is also in strong mutual reception sextile aspect to Venus (6), our most elevated body. These values, (5), (9) and (6) which show as the major aspecting values to the M.C. should be found in our selections. The number (9) horse with a total of (5) for the letters became my top selection. The I.D.'s for the horse, trainer and jockey totaled to (18) or (9). Of course the number (9) and the total for the letters (5) add to (14) or (5). The most elevated planet for this post time was Venus (6) and this value showed in the I.D. for the trainer with a total of (6) for the letters in his name.

Our second choice became the number (5) horse with an I.D. of (9). The (6) value showed in the I.D. for the jockey.

When the race was over, the number (9) horse won and the number (5) finished second. Both selections were (12) to (1) in the morning line but they appeared to have most of the right planetary values shown in their numbers. The results were more of a routine affair.

January 26th, 1977

Sixth Race   **Santa Anita**

Total	Number	Name	(Total Letters)	Trainer	Jockey	Morn. Line odds
(3)	(1)	FEATHERFOOT 8	(2)	Barrera 2	Pincay 8	3
	(2)	AUTHORIZATION 2	(4)	Proctor 8	Sanchez 6	10
Total (1)	(3)	ASCETIC 1 7 3	(7)	Cornell 2	Shoemaker 3	5/2
	(4)	MEDICAL MAN 4 4	(1)	Meeking 4	Pierce 8	8
	(5)	UDONEGOOD 1 3 1	(9)	Holt 8	Toro 4	9/2
	(6)	BEN S 2 1 5 3 6	(4)	Hine 8	Castaneda 2	4
	(7)	SWING THE HARBOR 6 9 8	(5)	Euster 1	McHargue 4	6

Post time for the (6th) found the following degrees on the cusps of our M.C. and Ascendant.

	Number Value
M.C. 22 degrees of Pisces	(3)
Asc. 9 degrees of Cancer	(2) and (7)
Aspects	**Number Value**
Jupiter sextile to the M.C.	(3)
Venus conjoined to the M.C.	(6)
Uranus trine to the ascendant	(6)

There are other aspects to the M.C. and ascendant but those shown above are the most pertinent because of this being the (6th) race with Libra falling on the cusp of the (6th) angle of our chart and ruled by Venus, our most elevated planetary body. When we project our (6th) angle cusp to the ascendant point we find (19) degrees of Capricorn falling on the cusp of the fourth angle, the end of the matter ruled by Saturn an (8) value. We also find Saturn's mutual reception factor, the Sun values (1) and (4) falling within the boundary of the (4th) angle.

In this race I gave preference to the number (1) horse with number value (8) shown for the I.D. The I.D.'s of the horse, trainer and jockey totaled to a (9) value. The number (1) post added to the number (2) shown for the total letters adds to our (3) value. Both the (9) and the (3) were in strong favorable aspect to the most elevated planet and prime race factor Venus, a (6) value. Of course the (2) total for the letters of the horse and the (2) I.D. for the trainer are symbolical of the Moon which was transiting Taurus ruled by Venus (6). The Jockey with the I.D. of (8) indicated that he should be in command of the situation at the end as this (8) value represents Saturn which rules Capricorn the sign which fell on the cusp of our (4th) angle projection. With the Sun, (1) and (4), posited in the (4th) in terms of Saturn (8), the number (1) horse with an I.D. of (8) I judged would win this race and it did.

The second selection became the number (3) horse with an I.D. of (1). The trainer, jockey, horse I.D.'s totaled to our prime race factor (6). The number (3) post added to the (7) for the total letters in the name of the horse nets to a (1) value, that of the Sun one of our prime end factors. This number (3) horse did finish second.

January 26th, 1977
Seventh Race   **Santa Anita**

	Number	Name	(Total Letters)	Trainer	Jockey	Morn. Line odds
	(1)	6 5 DUNCES WORLD 4 6	(2)	Heard 8	DiNicola 4	20
	(2)	1 1 6 T.V. TERESE 4 6 4	(8)	Mandella 4	McHargue 4	6
Total (8)	(3) ID4	8 6 GRACEFUL BANNER 2 2	(5)	Cofer 2	Olivares 2	8
	(4)	4 4 MISS RITZ 4 2	(8)	Nickerson 5	Pierce 8	20
	(5)	7 4 PLEASED LOOK 8 3	(2)	Canney 2	Mena 4	8
Total (6)	(6) ID8	5 4 SNOWY CAPE 6 2	(9)	Stute 6	Sellers 6	6
	(7)	4 3 4 OBEY THE HELM 6 9 8	(2)	Doyle 4	Lambert 3	15
	(8)	7 3 STELITA 2ND 6 6	(1)	Moreno 4	Castaneda 2	12
	(9)	2 1 7 I'M A CHARMER 1 1 8	(1)	Sacco 6	Howard 8	15
Total (1)	(10)	LOVELIEST 3	(9)	Pratt 8	Toro 4	3
	(11)	MIRACOLO 4	(8)	Mauro 4	Shoemaker 3	5
	(12)	TAISEERA 4	(8)	Cornell 2	Valdez 6	30

111

For the post time of the (7th) race we found the following degrees on the cusps of our angles.

	Number Value
M.C. 0 degrees of Aries value	(9)
Asc. 15 degrees of Cancer value	(2) and (7)

Aspects	**Number Value**
Sun sextile to the M.C.	(1) and (4)
Moon semi-sextile the M.C.	(2) and (7)
Mars opposed to the Asc.	(9)
Mercury opposed to the Asc.	(5)
Venus applying to sextile the Asc.	(6)
Jupiter applying to sextile the Asc.	(3)
Saturn semi-sextile to the Asc.	(8)

There are also aspects from Uranus, Neptune and Pluto but to mention them only duplicates the values shown above. At a quick glance we can see all our number factors, (1) through (9) are shown making aspects. However, our prime race factors are the (2) and the (7) as this is the (7th) race. Of course the solar body, making a prime aspect to the M.C., should be found in the selections values either directly, or, by strong aspect. In this case the Moon values (2) and (7) are in strong square aspect to the Sun (1) and (4). On the cusp of the (7th) angle of our chart we find Sagittarius, ruled by Jupiter (3). Neptune, a (5) value is posited in this (7th) angle. So, the number (3) horse with a total of (5) for the letters caught my eye in this race. Of course Jupiter (3) is conjoined to the Moon, values (2) and (7). When we check the I.D. for the horse we find a unit-force of (2) plus (2) which totals to our Sun value (4). The trainer and Jockey also show a (2) value for their I.D.'s. When we project the cusp of the (7th) angle to the ascendant we find (13) degrees of Aquarius falls on the cusp of the (4th) angle ruled by Saturn, an (8) value. In this position we find that Saturn has been elevated to the (10th) angle cusp, the most potent and preferential point of our wheel. When we add the number (3) post to the total of (5) for the letters in the selection's name, we total to our (8) value. Also when we total all the I.D.'s of this selection, we total to a (4) value for the horse, plus (2) for the trainer, plus (2) for the jockey and arrive at our (8) value. I picked this number (3) horse to win and it did.

My second choice became the morning line favorite at (3) to (1). It was running out of the number (10) post and showed an I.D. of (3) for the horse, an (8) for the trainer and a (4) value for the jockey, all prime factors for this race. With no (2) or (7) factors showing for this selection I had doubts about this horse winning, but, it did finish second.

January 26th, 1977

Eighth Race   **Santa Anita**

(San Vicente Stakes)   **(Purse $40,000.00)**

Number & Post

P.P.	No.	Name	(Total Letters)	Trainer	Jockey	Morn. Line odds
2	(1)	TEXT 4	(4)	Clyne 2	Pierce 8	4
Total (8) 9	(1-A)	REPLANT 2	(7)	McAnally 4	McHargue 4	4
1	(2)	HABITONY 8 1 5	(8)	Doyle 4	Shoemaker 3	2
3	(3)	INCREDIBLY LUCKY 1 3 7 7	(6)	Rettele 2	Lambert 3	12
Total (9) 4	(4)	CURRENT CONCEPT 2 2 6 6	(5)	Dutton 4	Pincay 8	4
5	(5)	CATHY'S REJECT 2 2 5 4	(3)	Manzi 4	Munoz 4	15
6	(6)	THREE BITS 9 2 2 3 1	(9)	Longden 3	Diaz 4	30
7	(7)	GO DON B 2 4 2	(6)	Holt 8	Olivares 2	8
8	(8)	SMASHER 3	(7)	Robbins 2	Toro 4	3

114

Post time for the (8th) race showed the following degrees on the cusps of our angles.

	Number Value
M.C. 15 degrees of Aries	(9)
Asc. 26 degrees of Cancer	(2) and (7)
Aspects	**Number Value**
Mars square the M.C.	(9)
Pluto opposed the M.C.	(9)
Neptune trine the M.C.	(5)
Saturn trine the M.C.	(8)
Venus trine the Asc.	(6)

In this (8th) race we find Saturn (8), our prime race value, making a favorable trine aspect to our M.C. As the prime planetary influence, the Sun values (1) and (4), is in strong mutual reception aspect to our (8) value, the number (1) and (4) horses commanded my attention in this race. Of course the number (1) horse was running out of the number (9) post position and the Mars (9) and Pluto (9) aspects to the M.C. gave added weight to this selection. Neptune (5) was also in favorable aspect to the M.C. and also to Saturn, value (8) our prime race factor. When we total the number (1) to the total letters (7) we add to (8), our prime race factor. When we add the (9) post to the number (1) and the total letters (7) we total to (17) or a net of (8).

It might be of help to mention here that when entries are coupled, as in this race, (1) and (1A), they are just considered as the same number. In this case (1) and ignore the letter (A).

On our (8th) angle cusp we find (27) degrees of Sagittarius, ruled by Jupiter (3). This value (3) is in mutual reception factor with Venus (6) our prime ascendant aspect to the ascendant for the time that this race was run. Jupiter (3) is also conjoined to the Moon, values (2) and (7) in Venus terms in Taurus, our money sign of the natural zodiac. This was the feature race of the day. The name of the race, (San Vicente Stakes), totals to a net of (7) for the letters. In our number (1) selection we find a total of (7) for the letters in its name and an I.D. of (2).

When we project the cusp of the (8th) angle to the ascendant point we find (13) degrees of Pisces ruled by Jupiter (3) falling on the cusp of the projected (4th) angle. We also find Venus (6), our mutual reception factor to Jupiter, posited in this angle. This projection also brings Pluto (9) into the preferential (10th) angle.

I judged that the number (1) horse, running out of the (9) post position would win this race. Jupiter (3) ruling the end of the matter was trine to Mars (9) conjoined to the Moon (2) and (7) and in parallel aspect to the Sun, (1) and (4), and Saturn, value (8). When we total the I.D.'s of the horse, trainer and jockey for the number (1) selection we net to (1), our prime race factor aspect.

The number (1) horse won and the number (4) finished second.

January 26th, 1977
Ninth Race

Santa Anita

Number & Post

	P.P.	No.	Name	(Total Letters)	Trainer	Jockey	Morn. Line odds
			4 5				
	6	(1)	MINI FALTA	(9)	Fanning	Olivares	5/2
			4 8		8	2	
	7	(1-A)	MAJINAI	(7)	Fanning	Pincay	5/2
			4		8	8	
Total			5 5				
(4)	1	(2)	SWIFT GYPSY	(1)	Potter	McHargue	5
	ID9		6 3		8	4	
			4 2 4				
	2	(3)	TURN OF FATE	(1)	Costello	Maese	12
			4 2 8		2	4	
	3	(4)	HEROICA	(7)	Mitchell	Munoz	15
			8		4	4	
			6 4				
	4	(5)	SILVER SLIP	(1)	Stute	Centeno	6
			6 6		6	6	
			5 6				
Total	5	(6)	SCOT'S DUNOON	(2)	Jones	Toro	4
(4)	ID1		6 4		3	4	
	8	(7)	RAFAGA	(6)	West	Calva	15
			2		6	2	
			8 4				
	9	(8)	LOUKHAL'S BEAU	(3)	Palma	Lambert	3
			3 2		8	3	
			6 1				
	10	(9)	TESSIE J	(7)	Whitby	Nogues	30
			4 3		6	5	

Post time for the (9th) race showed the following degrees on the cusps of our angles.

	Number Value
M.C. 25 degrees of Aries	(9)
Asc. 5 degrees of Leo	(1) and (4)
Aspects	**Number Value**
Venus semi-sextile the M.C.	(6)
Jupiter semi-sextile the M.C.	(3)
Sun opposed to the Asc.	(1) and (4)
Moon square to the Asc.	(2) and (7)

In this (9th) race we find our prime race factor Mars (9) exactly conjoined the (9th) angle cusp in Capricorn ruled by Saturn (8). Posited in this angle we find the Sun (1) and (4) which is our prime ascendant aspect at the time this race was run. Mars (9) was conjoined to Mercury (5), trine to Jupiter (3) and sextile to Venus (6). Jupiter and Venus are our closest M.C. aspecting bodies.

In this race my choice became the number (2) Horse running out of the number (1) post position. These numbers, the (1) and the (2) represent the two prime ascendant aspects of the Sun, (1) and (4) and the Moon, (2) and (7). This selection showed a (6) plus (3) which totaled to (9) for its I.D. These numbers represent our two main M.C. aspects and our prime race factor. This selection also showed a (5) plus (5) for the letters which totaled to (1). Mars (9) was conjoined to Mercury (5) on the cusp of the (9th) angle and the Sun (1) was posited in the (9th) angle. When we project the cusp of the (9th) angle to the ascendant point we find (21) degrees of Aries on the cusp of the (4th) with the Moon, (2) and (7), and Jupiter (3) conjoined in this angle and Mars (9) ruling the cusp. When we add the I.D.'s of the horse (9), trainer (8) and jockey (4) we total to (21) or a net of (3). This number (2) selection with a total of (3) for the total I.D.s did win this race.

The number (6) horse out of the (5) post position ran second. This horse showed a total of (2) for the letters and an I.D. of (1) for the horse our prime ascendant aspects at the time that this race was run.

It might be of interest to note here that there are other factors that come into play in work of this kind. I mention work because with all the numbers that we write on our program considerable effort and time is involved. The astrological knowledge is a must, but, it is not too difficult to master. But the other factors involve hunches and strong intuitive feelings that are generated through the experiences gained in the astrological practice. For instance, in reviewing our winning selections for the day's card, we can see at a glance considerable symbolism in each name.

In the first race we had a strong Saturn value (8) shown in the winning number. Also, the name, Doubtful Debbie, fits the symbolism. Doubt is a strong Saturn influence.

In the second race the Moon's symbolism in public appeal fits the name, Fly American. Its post position, number (7) and the total letters of (2) are the Moon's numbers. On the cusp of the second angle of our chart we find (27) degrees of Gemini. Not only do we repeat the moon's numbers in the degrees on the angle, but Gemini, ruled by Mercury is our zodiacal transportation house. Air travel is a form of transportation.

In the third race our number (3) comes into play and we look for a strong Jupiter (3) influence. In our chart for the day we can see at a glance that Jupiter is conjoined to the Moon. In the name of the number (2) horse we not only show the Moon's number (2) and (2) parts to the name, but, Jupiters optimism is symbolized in its name, Kid Konfidence.

In the fourth race, ruled by the Sun, our chart indicated a strong Saturn influence. The winning horse was named, The Fop. This means foolish person, or the equivalent. Saturn's influence is considered negative. Any person that manifests that trait is foolish. Of course this horse had an I.D. of (8) which gave us our clue.

In the fifth race our winning horse was named, Thirteenth Hope. Our (5th) angle of the natural Zodiac rules gambling and speculation. Thirteen is considered lucky or unlucky from one's point of view. Also, when we gamble we hope, — to win of course. This name belonged to the number (9) horse and Mars (9) was conjoined to Mercury (5) in our chart. On the

cusp of the (5th) angle of our chart is (13) degrees of Virgo,
ruled by Mercury (5). Could anything be better symbolized?

In the (6th) race, symbolized by Venus, our winning horse
was named, Featherfoot. He showed number (1) on his saddle
cloth. On the cusp of the (6th) angle we show (21) degrees of
Libra, ruled by Venus. At the time that this race was run, Venus
was conjoined to the M.C. Venus is an artistic influence and
dancing is one of its talents. The use of the feet and our name
Featherfoot symbolize this grace. The total of (2) for the letters
and the (1) post add to (3), a Jupiter value and the prime mutual
aspect to our most elevated Venus astride the M.C. when this
race was run. Of course the (21) degrees of Libra adds (2) plus
(1) to our (3). In this race the number (3) horse ran second and
its name was, Ascetic, also quite fitting for its post number (3).
Jupiter (3) rules Sagittarius our religious angle of the natural
zodiac.

In the (7th) race we use the Moon (2) and (7) as our prime
race factors. This lunar body is conjoined to Jupiter (3) in the
(12th) angle of our chart. In the name of the winner of the (7th)
race, Graceful Banner, we find considerable symbolism. Our
(7th) angle has about (3) degrees of Sagittarius on the cusp
which gives us Jupiter (3) as its ruler. Jupiter is in strong mutual
reception sextile aspect to Venus, our planetary value of grace.
The Moon is indicative of the public or public functions where
pennants and banners are used. So, we can see that this number
(3) horse, Graceful Banner, fits all our symbolism. Our second
finisher in this race was named, Loveliest, with an I.D. of (3)
and good symbolism for this race.

In the (8th) race the winning horse was named, Replant.
Scorpio, the natural (8th) angle of the zodiac is symbolized by
energy and sex. Regeneration is one of its keywords. This horse
with (7) for a total of its letters plus the number (1) post totals
to our number (8). This number (8) is also our eternity symbol
which denotes continuity, as does replanting.

In the (9th) race we use number (9) as our prime significator.
This is Mars number and Mars was conjoined to Mercury (5)
on the cusp of the (9th) angle of our chart. Mercury is our
communication and transportation symbol and Mars is our

energy symbol. The name of the winning horse had (2) parts to it with (5) letters in each part. Mercury's influence is sometimes dual in nature. The winged heel of Mercury conveys speed in its symbolism. In this race it was quite fitting that our winner should be named Swift Gypsy, with an I.D. of (9).

From the foregoing descriptions of the astrological numerical factors of: As above, so below, we can see considerable consistency. In this work a direct Mercury helps, as one must be accurate in one's figures. Good personal directions help sharpen the intuitive factor. But just a rudimentary knowledge of astrology and numbers can work wonders.

In application of this work for daily use, exactness of degree is not a prime requisite. Just an application to the degree of an aspect will work. Just a similar sign position can be considered as a conjunction.

The tropical zodiacal application becomes the base for all of this work. Yet, the author believes that astrology and numbers are spiritual and mental symbols that aid one in postulating mental abstractions, and, much of this is beyond the kin of mortals.

Chapter 12
The Zodiac and the New Testament

In this chapter I think that it is quite appropriate to consider the English language bible in terms of: As above, so below. This being chapter (12), or (3), we should have some religious interpretation. Jupiter, value (3), is the accepted ruler of the (9th) angle of our zodiac, which governs amongst other things, religion and higher learning. Jupiter also rules the (12th) angle, that of limitation.

In our Holy Bible, in the New Testatment, we note; Holy, (4) letters, and Bible, (5) letters, add to a total of (9) for the letters. This book is for all of humanity, symbolical of the (9) orifices of the human species. The words New, (3) letters, and Testament, (9) letters, total to (12), or (3). When we total the (9) for our Holy Bible to the (3) for the New Testament, we still get our (3) value, that of Jupiter, ruler of the angle of religion in the heavenly zodiac. So, this section of our Holy Bible, that of the New Testament, should cover that which we seek in our religious interpretation.

One might postulate the question; — Why the New Testament, when the Old Testament adds to the same number of letters? To answer that question we have only to call upon our phonetic values of the words (new) and (old). The word (new) shows a phonetic value net of (2). When we add the (2) to the total of the letters (3), we total to (5). The (5) is the symbol of Mercury which symbolizes a message, or, communication which we are seeking in the relationship of the Zodiac and Religion.

The word (old) totals to a phonetic net of (4). When we add the (4) to the total of the letters (3), we total to (7). This (7) is our Lunar symbol of fullness which would in this instance infer the complete activity of our Zodiac. The (4) being our builder's symbol of activity and the (3) being our growth and wisdom symbol which results in the fullness, or, fulfillment (7) of the zodiacal activity. The (4) elements of fire, air, earth and water, together with the (3) triplicities of the zodiacal wheel make for this complete fulfillment.

In the first book of Moses called Genesis, the word (Genesis) totals to (7) letters. Also the first sentence; In the beginning God created the heaven and the earth, — we total to (44) for the letters, which in turn adds (4) plus (4) to (8). The (8) is our symbol of eternity, or, eternal. The phonetic values of this first sentence also nets to a (4). When we total these activity symbols they add (8) plus (4) to (12), the number of signs of the Zodiac. The (12) adds (1) plus (2) to (3), our Jupiter value ruler of the (9th) angle of our zodiac, that of religion. Also we can note that it is the mating of the positive (1) and the negative (2) that produces the growth and the wisdom that is symbolized by this number (3). This first sentence in the King James version of our Holy Bible actually does convey the tremendous truth that we are in an eternal (8) process of activity (4) and growth (3).

Jupiter (3) rules both the (9th) and (12th) angles of our zodiac, higher learning and limitation. We usually seek divine guidance when we exhaust all physical means. Note that divine, (6) letters, and guidance, (8) letters, add (6) plus (8) to (14), or, (5), our communication number, being the value of Mercury (5).

In the Holy Bible, in the New Testament, we find in Matthew, (7) letters, (6th) chapter, verses, (9), (10), (11), (12) and (13) our communication, and answer. When we add our (5) verses, they total to (55), or, (10), or, (1). When we continue our addition of letters, chapter and verses, we total (7) plus (6) plus (1) equals a total of (14), or, (5). Again we have our communication number. And, what do we find in these (5) verses? None other than The Lord's Prayer! Again we can add, — The, (3) letters, Lord's, (5) letters, and Prayer, (6) letters, (3) plus (5) plus (6) equals (14), or, (5).

Mercury, value (5), is the closest planetary body to the Sun. The Sun rules the (5th) angle of our zodiac and also rules the heart, (5) letters, in the human body. The (5th) angle rules off-spring, or, children amongst other things. Jesus, (5) letters, also known as the Son of God, advises amongst other things, to pray from the heart.

We find this advice in chapters (5), (6) and (7), which add to (18), or, (9), the number of humanity, in Christ's Sermon on the Mount. We can also note again that our (9th) angle of our zodiac rules religion or higher learning. When we add Christ's, (7) letters, Sermon, (6) letters, On, (2) letters, The, (3) letters, and Mount, (5) letters, we total to (23), or, (5) our communication number.

The Lord's Prayer is our divine communication. We can note that when we add all the letters of The Lord's Prayer plus the total for the numbers of the verses, which is (256) plus (1) we get (257), or, (14), or, (5), which is the official printed King James version of our English language Holy Bible. Mercury, value (5), becomes the key, (3) letters, which conveys the message. When we run up against physical limitations, we are advised to pray from the heart for divine guidance.

The five verses which contain the divine communication are, (9), (10), (11), (12), and (13), which add to (55), or, (10), or, (1). This number (1) is the number of completeness and also a symbol of authority. This prayer we have from good authority, covers all of our human needs.

The first sentence; Our Father which art in heaven, Hallowed be thy name, has a total of (42) letters, or, a net of (6). This is Venus value (6) and is the symbol of harmony and love. It is through love that all flourishes. So, in the first sentence we seek harmony through love, and, we have been advised, through the sermon on the mount, to seek through the heart.

In verse (10) we state; Thy kingdom come. Thy will be done in earth, as it is in heaven. This verse totals (48) letters, or, (12), or (3). This is Jupiter's value (3) and our principal of growth. This verse indicates that we grow through divine wisdom.

In verse (11); Give us this day our daily bread. This is an appeal for sustenance. This sentence has a total of (26) letters, or, (8). This is Saturn's value (8). It is a symbol of limitation. So, in this statement we acknowledge our physical limitations.

In verse (12) we state; And forgive us our debts, as we forgive our debtors. In this statement we have a total of (41) letters, or,

(5). This is Mercury's number (5), and, amongst its terms is that of reason, as well as communication. Here we seek forgiveness through communicating our rational thought that if we forgive, we shall be forgiven.

In verse (13) we state; And lead us not into temptation, but deliver us from evil; For thine is the kingdom, and the power, and the glory, forever. A-men. This is the largest verse and its letters total to (99), or, (18), or, (9). This is our total human number of humanity (9), also that of Mars. It is indicative of desire and human frailties. In our closing statement we acknowledge the divine authority and ask for guidance.

So, in using this prayer we find a complete process for our living. For if we can manifest, in our daily lives, these (5) principles of Love, growth, sustenance, forgiveness and guidance, and, seek the kingdom first, then all things shall be added to us.

If we add the principals of love, (4) letters, growth, (6) letters, sustenance, (1) letters, forgiveness, (2) letters, and guidance, (8) letters, we total to (21), or, (3). This is Jupiter's value of growth which rules our (9th) angle of higher learning, or, divine wisdom.

The Lord's Prayer, total of (5) letters thus becomes the key, (3) letters. In the name Jesus Christ we get, Jesus, (5) letters, Christ, (6) letters, which add (5) plus (6) equals (2). The (5) is Mercury's number of communication. The (6) is Venus' number of love. The (2) is the Moon's number, indicative of the masses. So, in this name we have a message of love for humanity.

The word love, (4) letters, is the number of the Sun, which rules the heart, (5) letters. When we add the (4) plus the (5) we total to (9), which is the number of humanity. Also our Holy, (4) letters, and Bible, (5) letters when added total to our (9) value. Again we have a message from the heart for humanity.

As a closing note for this chapter we might note that the word love, which totals to (4) letters also has a phonetic value of (2). This is a lunar value denoting personal, human influence of the masses of humanity. The (4) plus the (2) totals to the (6) value of Venus, the zodiacal symbol of love. This love value is slightly different when applied to the name of Christ. Here we have a (6) letter name with a (6) phonetic value as well. When we add the (6) plus the (6) we total to our (3). This is our Jupiter value (3), the greater fortune of our zodiac which manifests as the wisdom principal. So, the name Christ symbolizes the love, wisdom principal.

Venus, value (6), a monetary as well as our love principal, is exalted in the (12th) angle of our zodiac, ruled by Jupiter, (3), and blends harmoniously with the growth principal. On the mundane scene our assets are banked and our credit expands through the (9th) angle of our zodiac and this makes for greater fortunes. So also is our divine estate advanced through the love wisdom principal of Jupiter (3), our greater fortune ruler of the (9th) and (12th) angles of our zodiac.

Chapter 13
Superstition, Accidents and Fate

This chapter appropriately numbered, thirteen, I have devoted to recounting a couple of major disasters, which proved to be good examples of the Astro-Numerical geographical application.

Quite a few folks classify the science of astrology as superstition, mostly because of the ridicule bestowed upon the subject, without giving it a fair investigation. What we don't know, we tend to fear. Things that happen, for which one does not have an explanation, one tends to term as an accident. That which happens beyond our present control, one tends to call fate. Yet, when our knowledge increases, superstition becomes myth, and, wisdom can bestow blessings through intelligent living. So, the so-called accidents and fate become nothing more than the law of cause and effect in operation.

On April 18th, 1906, in San Francisco, my father had a rude awakening about 5:00 A.M. He remembered this event well, because it was the date of the worst earthquake that he had ever experienced. The furniture in his bedroom, bounced, shook and toppled. The house was shaken off of its foundation, and, outside, the street opened up, water mains broke and the steel rails in the street buckled. Then on top of that, fire broke out, and, burned for several days. Most folks slept out of doors for days, and, after-shocks were many.

I am writing about this event, because it not only struck close to home, but, it is a classic example of an unfortunate happening perfectly shown by the astro-numerical process of; As above, so below.

San Francisco totals to, (12) or (3) letters, and, is located about (122) degrees west longitude, and, about (38) north latitude. The big show began on a Wednesday, Mercury's day, about 5:00 A.M. in San Francisco where Neptune, a 5 value, conjoined the M.C. at longitude (122) west, which totals to (5). The latitude of San Francisco, (3) letters, is (38) north, or, (3) Plus (8) totals to (11) or (2). The Moon (2) was in Pisces (3) conjoined to Saturn (8). The total date of 4-18-1906 adds (4) plus (9) plus (7) to a total of (20) or (2). Mercury, value (5) was in Mars' fire sign Aries, a (9) value, retrograde to stationary and in square aspect to Neptune (5) conjoined the M.C., Capricorn with an (8) value.

At the time of this event, we had (5) planets, Mercury (5), Neptune (5), Uranus (6), Jupiter (3) and Saturn (8) all making the (90) degree, or, (9) aspect to each other, when (9) degrees of Capricorn reached the M.C. These planetary values when added (5) plus (5) plus (6) plus (3) plus (8) total (27), or, (9). Remember all this was happening on the (18th) which adds to (9). This is Mars number which denotes fire and violence. In this event the fire did more damage than the earthquake which caused the fire.

In geographical location we find that San Francisco is located on the cusp of Sagittarius. This is a fire sign and the people of this city have been fire and quake conscious ever since.

San Francisco has a phonetic value of (4). This (4) is the symbol of the square, and, it is also the builder's symbol. This city was rebuilt and is one of the world's most beautiful cities.

The Moon values (2) and (7) add to (9). This body is considered as the second hand of the cosmic clock. When this body reached the cusp of Pisces, a (3) value, it was within orb of conjunction with Saturn, an (8) value, which ruled the M.C. at this particular hour. It also reached the orb of square, (90) degrees, or, (9) of Jupiter, value (3). At this point the Moon paralleled the Sun, values (1) and (4). San Francisco, (3) total letters and phonetic value of (4), became ripe for this event, as ripe as the tomato with the ear phones, and, — it sure was a big one!

The earthquake caused a lot of damage, including the fire, but, there was more fire damage. The Moon conjoined to Saturn, the M.C.'s ruler, showed why. The Moon rules liquids, and, conjoined to Saturn tended to limit the water available to fight the fire. In this instance, with all the (9) energy, and, Mars ruling fire, the fire fighters had to back fire. Fight fire with fire, because of the lack of sufficient water.

Our next event is one that occurred on a Sunday evening, April 14th, 1912. Here we have a date that went into the marine disaster records as one to be long remembered. Late that evening, the steamship Titanic, of the White Star shipping firm, hit an iceberg in the north Atlantic and sank carrying 1,517 souls to the world beyond.

I have selected this event as my classic example of a marine tragedy because it happened in time of peace, not war, and, could have been averted.

On this date, the (14th) which adds to (5), Mercury, value (5) was retrograde and combust the Sun, values (1) and (4), in the Mars' fire sign Aries, a (9) value. These two bodies were in adverse square aspect to Neptune, value (5), in the water sign Cancer ruled by the Moon, values (2) and (7) which total (9). The Moon on this date was transiting the water sign Pisces, value (3), ruled by Jupiter, value (3), and in square aspect to Jupiter, which was retrograde in the fire sign Sagittarius, value (3). Also on this date Mars, value (9) was in its fall sign, Cancer, ruled by the Moon and was in square aspect to Venus, value (6), transiting Mars' fire sign Aries.

Aries is the first sign of the natural zodiac. This was the maiden voyage of this luxury liner. It has been stated that this ship was trying to establish a new crossing record. Whether this is true or not, this date was not a propitious one for such a steamship in this particular area. We can note that this ship departed from the geographical zodiacal area ruled by Aries and Mars. It met its tragic end in the geographical area ruled by Pisces and Jupiter, the Atlantic Ocean. The Moon was transiting Pisces, which rules this area and was in adverse aspect to Jupiter, the ruler of Pisces. All this happened when Mercury, value (5), which rules communication and transportation was retrograde and combust (adverse aspect) the Sun, in the fire sign Aries.

The name of the steamship, Titanic, shows a total of (7) letters and a phonetic value of (9). When we add these two values we get (16) or (7). This is a Moon number. The name of the place where it all happened, the Atlantic, shows a total of (8) letters and a phonetic value of (3). When we add these two values (8) plus the (3) we get (11) or (2). This also is a Moon number. This ship went to the bottom of the Atlantic in the early morning hours of Monday, considered as the Moon's day, with values (2) and (7) assigned to it. When we total the two numbers of the ship and the place (7) plus the (2) we total to (9). This is Mars number which rules Aries, value (9), the sign containing the retrograde Mercury combust to the Sun.

This tragedy occurred at night during the dark of the Moon, which covered (2) dates, April 14, 1912 and April 15, 1912. These dates add to (4) and (5) respectively, which in turn add (4) plus (5) to a total of (9). As we have shown this is Mars number (9) which rules the fire sign Aries, where Mercury (5) and the Sun (4) were conjoined. This ship had its side ripped open when it struck the iceberg on the (14th) which adds to (5). It sank on 4-15-1912, which totals to a net of (5). We can also note that 1,517 people lost their lives, or, (1) plus (5) plus (1) plus (7) totals to (14) or (5). This ship went down before help could reach the area. When the water, ruled by the Moon, reached the boilers, ruled by Mars, there was a large explosion and the ship settled to the bottom of the Atlantic.

In closing our comment on this ill-fated event, we might note that the company's name also fitted this experience. White, (5) letters, Star, (4) letters, add to a total of (9). Mercury, value (5), was retrograde and combust the Sun, Values (1) and (4) which add to (5) and rules the (5th) angle of the zodiac, in Aries ruled by Mars, value (9). The phonetic value of White (2) and Star (4) when added total to (6). When we add the letters (9) to the phonetic (6) we total to (15) or (6). This is Venus value (6) and we noted that Mars was in adverse aspect to Venus. Saturn, the planet of karma and destiny was transiting Taurus, ruled by Venus, value (6).

The thing that did the ship in, the iceberg, totals to (7) letters, with a phonetic value of (5). When we total these two factors we get (12) or (3). The iceberg reflects all the factors in this incident. The (7) letters matches the (7) letters in the name

Titanic. The (5) phonetic value matches the retrograde Mercury, value (5). The (12) matches the (12th) sign of the zodiac, Pisces, which geographically rules the area and the (3) matches the Jupiter value (3) which rules Pisces and was in square aspect to the Moon.

Another date that most folks will be able to remember occurred on August 6th, 1945. Here we had an (8th) month and a (6th) day and a (1) year which when added (8) plus (6) plus (1) totals to (15) or (6). This (6) value is symbolical of Venus, and, it is also the number we have assigned to Uranus, the higher octave of Venus. On this day, a Monday, values (2) and (7) which total to (9), Mars, value (9), was conjoined to Uranus, value (6), at about (9) degrees of Gemini, value (5). This malefic conjunction fell in the exact degree of Uranus' placement in the United States 1776 birth chart. Mercury, value (5), had been retrograde, in relation to the earth's motion, but, on this day, was almost stationary about to move direct again. This is a critical period for judgements and news evaluation. It was on this Monday in August, that the United, (6) letters, States, (6) letters, which add to a total of (12) or (3), notified Japan, (5) letters with a phonetic value of (9), that if it did not surrender, a terrible bomb would wipe out one of their cities. The news media said that this action was taken to; End, (3) letters, The, (3) letters, War, (3) letters, which when added totals to (9). Jupiter, value (3), representing the United States, (6) plus (6) letters total to (3), was conjoined to Mercury (5) in Virgo (5), the scientific research sign ruled by Mercury. The message was not heeded, Mercury stationary, and, the first Atomic, (6) letters, Device, (6) letters, was exploded over Hiroshima, (9) letters.

The Sun, values (1) and (4), on this day was transiting its own sign Leo, values (1) and (4). This (1st) event of its kind, in our time, aptly describes the fire-ball that resulted in the exact geographical location on the planet earth. Leo falls over Japan. This was done in the interest of peace, (5) letters. Mercury (5) was in negative terms and the experience was not believed.

Three days later on August (9th), 1945, an (8) month, a (9) day and a (1) year, which adds to (18) or (9), a second device was exploded, this time on Nagasaki, (8) total letters, and, a phonetic value of (1), which adds (8) plus (1) equals (9). On this day, Mercury (5), was moving forward again and the message got through to Japan (5) letters with a phonetic value of (9).

The death and destruction on the (9) day and total date which added to (9), indicated by Mars (9) conjoined to Uranus (6) was in the interest of peace. This second, (6) letters, device, (6) letters, was exploded, (8) letters, over Nagasaki, (8) letters, when the Sun, values (1) and (4), was in exact sextile aspect to Uranus, value (6). Our longitude (130) east, (1) plus (3) plus (0) totals to (4), the Sun's value. Our latitude (33) north adds, (3) plus (3) a (6) value, that of Uranus. The Sun was still transiting Leo which rules this part of the globe.

All this happened on a Thursday, Jupiter's day value (3). This planet is considered the greater fortune and it was conjoined to Mercury in the Mercury sign of Virgo. The news was celebrated through-out the world. But, the aftermath is something else. We still fear the unknown. The atom is still the big mystery, and, it is feared all the more today by the ecologists and many members of the establishment. Perhaps as we break the mental barriers and learn to live more intelligently, our fears will subside.

In our most recent event, a plane tragedy, we note that again we run into the double unit force of the number (9). For on March 27, 1977, we have a (9) day and a (9) for the total added date. This is Mars' number as we have noted and this influence can be hot, fiery and violent. This is especially so when the square, or, critical aspects are in effect.

On this day the Moon squared the Sun, and, the Sun was in Mars' sign of fire, Aries, conjoined to Mercury the transportation symbol. Saturn was also making a strong square aspect to Uranus. Saturn, the planet of fate was in the Sun's sign and Uranus was in the negative angle of Mars, that of Scorpio. All this tends to add fire to the Mars potential. The planet Mars was in the astrological sign Pisces. This geographical location, as we have noted in a previous chapter, falls over the Atlantic Ocean. The Canary Islands, where the tragedy occurred, are located in the Atlantic Ocean.

According to the news account, a bomb was exploded at Las Palmas airport. As a precautionary measure, the two planes, that were eventually involved in the accident, were detoured to the Santa Cruz airport on the island of Tenerife. We can note that the (2) planes were (747)'s, which add (7) plus (4) plus (7) to (18) or (9), which is Mars number. The accident occurred in the Atlantic in the geographical rulership of Pisces. Mars, number (9), was transiting Pisces at the time of the crash, or, mishap. Also Las Palmas, (9) letters was the name of the original destination of the (2) (747)'s, which total to (9) and the place where the bomb was exploded to cause their rerouting. Santa Cruz, where the accident occurred, also has a total of (9) letters in its name. The island of Tenerife has (8) letters in its name with a phonetic value of (4) which totals (8) plus (4) equals (3). This is the sign and area of the Mars transit, Pisces, value (3). Its longitude is (17) west, or a net of (8). Its latitude is (28) north, or, (2) plus the (8) totals to (10), or, (1). When we total the longitude and the latitude, (8) plus the (1) we total to (9). This island, or, area in the Atlantic ruled by Pisces where Mars was transiting was ripe for the action.

In reading the news account of this tragedy, the article mentioned the previous biggest disaster in aviation history. That one occurred near Paris, (5) letters, on March 3rd, 1974, which adds (3) plus (3) plus (3) to a total of (9). On this date Mercury, value (5), was retrograde. Mars, Saturn and the Moon make a forbidding combination, especially in the transportation sign, Gemini, ruled by Mercury, when in parallel aspect, and, when Mercury was retrograde.

I believe that the foregoing accounts of the mundane happenings are sufficient to give the readers a hint as to the whys and wherefores. Too much dwelling upon these negative aspects is not good.

One can, if one chooses, through the use of the astro-numerical factors, make life a little less stressful by selecting more propitious periods and thereby enjoy life that much more.

Chapter 14
Cabala and Alchemy

Somewhere in a recent magazine article, I read a very profound item about Christianity and Alchemy. This piece mentioned that alchemical speculations, of one kind or another, have existed from the beginning of recorded history. Chemistry, the science of the land of Khem, Egypt, was first used as a spiritual, or, philosophical art, and, as such, achieved considerable respectability in the Christian world.

In this article, it mentioned that Trithemius was a profound student of the cabala and the mysteries of Christian Alchemy. This personality viewed, or, depicted God as a mysterious and hidden fire, present in all existing things. This fire generated all things and will continue to do so throughout all eternity. No fire can burn and no light can appear in the natural world without the addition of air, which, makes the combustion possible. This air, called divine breath, is referred to as the Holy Spirit. This breath sustains the fire within the soul so that the light will appear, and, be nourished by the fire. This light was described as love, gladness and joy abiding with the eternal one. This light was called Christ. Those who have not this light within themselves have only a burning fire. But if this light is of Christ, one so illumined, will know and recognize the light of Christ as it exists in all of nature. All things, therefore, are made up of a trinity; fire, light and air. In the natures of all creatures the fire is the Father; the light is the Son and the Holy Spirit is the nourisher and mover.

When we consider the fire, light and air in the terms of our Astro-Numerical cabala for the English language, the results tend to support a compatible interpretation. In applying the cabala for our word interpretation, we use the total letters and the total phonetic and add these two values to a single digit. To get an understanding of a group of words, we combine the process.

Fire has a total of (4) letters and the phonetic values total to (12) or (3). When we add the (4) plus the (3) we total to a (7). With the knowledge of our astrology we intuitively interpret as follows: The (4) is the builder's symbol of the Sun which makes the whole wheel of our zodiac. This (4) also represents the (4) triplicities of our zodiac. The phonetic value (3) is our growth symbol. By the addition of the two values we get our full Moon number (7). This (7) then is symbolical of the seven planetary values that make for all the activity in our wheel. So, the Sun, the fire, is the source. Note that in the (4) there is only the negative value of the source, the Sun. The first principle, symbolized by number (1) does not appear in any of the totals. The God principle is the hidden factor found only in the individual parts that make up the total. The first principle is acknowledged as unknowable, except as through its working parts.

The word air has a total of (3) letters with a phonetic value of (3). When we add the (3) plus (3) we total to a (6). It is mentioned that air is needed to make combustion possible. Here we have the double factor of the growth principle (3). We are advised that we not only experience growth as a natural necessity, but, through its action is generated love. Love is the influence of Venus, value (6). This air, or, divine breath, is called the Holy Spirit, a breath which sustains the fire within the soul so that the light will appear and be nourished by the fire, and this light is called love. We can also note that the words, divine breath are (6) plus (6) letters which total to (3). This matches our factors that make up our description of the word air, (3) plus (3) which total to (6). The (6) plus (6) is a love principle combined to the wisdom principle, also symbolical of the (3), a Jupiter value. The (3) plus (3) is a growth principle combined to the love principle, Venus a (6) value of the lesser fortune, as it is known in the astrological lore. It is also a lower step to a higher one, from love to wisdom.

When we consider our third word of the trinity, light, we find that it totals to (5) letters. This is our communication number. When we relate love we sustain the fire, the Christ light within the heart, or, the Christ principle in all things. The word light has a phonetic value of (8). This is Saturn's symbol of the; Ring pass not, or, limitation principle of our solar system. Note that this phrase; Ring pass not, adds (4) plus (4) plus (3) to a total of (11) or (2) letters. This is a Moon value and symbolizes the physical manifestation. The Moon is a secondary principle in relation to the Sun, which symbolizes a primary principle. The phonetic total of; Ring pass not, is a (9) value. This is the number of humanity and the sum total of our number system. When we add the total letters to the total phonetic we total a (2) value. So, this limitation pertains to the physical manifestation. When we add the total letters of the word light, to its phonetic value we total (5) plus (8) to (13) or (4). This is the negative number of the Sun. Our physical Sun is a reflector of the spiritual Sun. This (4) principle then refers to the physical light. It is the builder's symbol. So, in the physical realm, light is the first principle of creation. The fire, our Sun, creates the light, which, in turn, resulted in our solar system and our earth with its atmosphere, air, and, physical life.

When we total the totals shown for our fire, light and air, we add (7) plus (4) plus (6) which totals to (17) or (8). Again we get our Saturn symbol, (8), that of limitation. We have noted in a previous chapter how this (8) symbol is created by tracing the Chaldean order of Planetary hours and rulerships through the zodiacal wheel. This (8) symbol, amongst other things, is our symbol of infinity and eternity.

The article mentioned that all things are made of this trinity; fire, light and air. Also, that this mysterious, hidden fire called, God, has generated this trinity and will continue throughout all eternity.

We might at this point consider the word, God, in the light of our English cabala. We find that it has a total of (3) letters, symbolical of growth and also of the trinity. The phonetic value totals to our (8) symbol. When we total the (3) to the (8) we get (11) or (2). The (8) is our symbol of eternity and limitation. The (2) value pertains to earth and human values. So, the word God in the English language is a human attempt to identify deity. It is factual in so far as describing the eternal trinity and its growth principle, but, it still remains as a mystery.

When we use the term spirit and add the letters, we total to (6). This is the Venus symbol of love. It has often been said that God is love. The phonetic value of spirit is (4). This is the builder's symbol of the Sun, the source of the fire. When we add the total letters to the phonetic total we get (6) plus (4) equals (10) or (1). This is the prime source number of the Sun. This is the number of the individual, or, the One, or, a beginning. We might say that this number symbolizes everything, or, consciousness. To elaborate more on this one would have to practice the Art of Meditation. We are informed that through the practice of meditation, by Yogananda, through his book, Autobiography of a Yogi, that, this is the only way to become aware of the divine being. Words, (5) letters, Mercury's symbol, are still only communicative factors.

At this point in our book it might be of interest to consider a few words that we use in our Astro-Numerological work in the light of our English cabala. I will try to give a reasonable interpretation of the names of the planets and signs of our zodiac so that the readers may gain a little better understanding of their usage and meaning.

Starting with the names of the planets of our zodiac, we find that these differ from the numbers assigned to them. However, in analyzing them through our English language cabala, they do match rulerships and symbolism through their total letters, phonetic values and total digits.

Starting with the Sun, which shows a total of (3) letters, we have a symbol of wisdom and growth. The phonetic values total to (13) or (4). This is the builder's symbol. When we add the (3) plus the (4) we total to (7). This is the full Moon symbol of fruition. In this case the (4) elements, fire, air, earth and water added to the (3) triplicities indicate the fullness of the (7) planetary values to complete all our zodiac activity. In our analysis of the word, fire, we came up with the same numerical values, (4) plus (3) to get our (7). This is a natural correlation of the Sun to fire, and, fire to the Sun.

Next we can consider the name, Moon. Here we have a total

of (4) letters. Again, we have the builder's symbol, and, this building principle manifests in the (4) phases of the Moon. New, first quarter, full, and last quarter. The phonetic value adds to (6). This is Venus number symbolical of the feminine principle and females. The Moon and Venus have considerable influence on females. When we add the (4) plus the (6) we total to a (1) value. This (1) is symbolical of the complete lunar cycle. The (27) day lunar cycle corresponds to the (27) day menstrual function of the female of the human species. Of course all growth, through the love aspect of the Venus influence, also makes for the complete cycle of the lunar influence on all growing things. Every lunation effects all matters accordingly, mineral, or, organic, and this is a very important base of astrology. Venus' sign, Taurus, is also the exaltation sign of the Moon.

Mercury totals to (7) letters. This is symbolical of all the (7) planetary influences. This planet, as we have noted, takes on the quality of the sign and planet in closest aspect with it. This (7) is also the full Moon number. Mercury and the Moon have considerable influence on the mental faculties. The phonetic values total to (19) or (1). This is the primary number of the Sun and this planet is in closest orbit to the Sun. When we total the letters and the phonetic, we get (7) plus (1) equals an (8) value. This is Saturn's number of limitation, or, restriction. This (8) symbol is a cold calculating aspect and one is cautioned to be unemotional when reasoning. Yet, even in this reasoning, there is limitation. We cannot entirely let the head rule the heart, the source of all wisdom. So, one can conclude that knowledge and wisdom are as different as day and night, symbolized by the Sun (1) and the Moon (7) factors which make up the total (8). The knowledge through the Saturn symbol (8), as we have shown in a previous chapter, must pass the test of the heart.

Venus, adds to a total of (5) letters. This planet is the love influence of our zodiac and the affairs of the (5th) angle include those of the heart. This (5th) angle is ruled by the Sun, values (1) and (4) which total (5). The phonetic value of Venus totals to (20) or (2). This is the Moon value and we have noted that the Moon is exalted in the Venus sign Taurus. When we total the (5) plus the (2) we get the full Moon number (7). This number tends to accentuate the Moon, Venus relationship mostly through the full Moon house, or, angle of our zodiac, that of the (7th) which rules partnerships and the spouse. Here the love principle manifests through love of others.

Saturn's total letters add to (6), and, the phonetic values add to (20) or (2). We have just described the relationship between the (2) and the (6) values of the Moon and Venus. We have noted that they are both feminine and that Venus is the love influence. When we total the (2) and the (6), we get our (8) value of Saturn. So we might say that Saturn is also a strong love influence through the discipline of the awareness of limitation. A symbol of chastity. Karma, a Saturn symbol, is not considered evil. It is an opportunity to face up to situations which make for spiritual growth. Note that karma has (5) letters and a phonetic value of (1). When we total these two figures we total (6). This is a love influence through discipline.

Jupiter, the greater fortune, totals to (7) letters. The phonetic values total to a (7) as well. When we total the (7) plus (7) we total to (14) or (5). Perhaps this is where we get the term greater fortune, from the words attributed to Shakespeare. (There is a tide in the affairs of men, which, when seized at the flood, leads on to greater fortune.) The flood is the symbol of the full Moon. The (7) is the full Moon number. In this name we find a double unit force of (2) sevens. The total of the two sevens, (14) is made up of the two numbers of the Sun, the prime body of the zodiac. When we add the (1) and the (4) we total to (5). The Sun rules the (5th) angle of the zodiac, that of love and speculation, and, off-spring. Success in these affairs is usually considered most fortunate.

Mars totals to (4) letters, and this is the negative number of the Sun, the builder's symbol. The phonetic value also totals to (4). So we have a unit of force of a negative value which when added totals to (8). The Sun is exalted in Aries, the first sign of the zodiac, ruled by Mars, value (9). Mars also rules the (8th) angle of the zodiac, that of Scorpio. The force in this name is powerful and the planetary body is noted for energy and force. Much discipline, symbolized by the planetary value (8), is required to use this force constructively. The (4) is the symbol of the square and we have noted that it is a (90) degree or (9) aspect, and is considered adverse. This is so because of the double unit of force noted in this name. Most folks cannot handle this much force. When the individual learns the discipline to handle this much energy, then much constructive effort can be had in the (4) plus (4) builder's power.

The name Uranus totals to (6) letters. This is the love symbol and this planet is considered the higher octave of Venus, value (6). The love principle here is a higher octave of the personal love of Venus. It is considered altruistic, and, is symbolized as brotherhood. The phonetic values total to (23) or (5). This is the mental symbol of Mercury, value (5), but, here it goes a step beyond the reasoning mind and is indicative of the intuitive factor. When we add the (6) plus the (5) we total to (11) or (2). This is a Moon value, the new Moon symbol. Uranus planetary value deals with eccentricity. New fads, ideas, ideals and things much beyond the established culture. Also the influence of this body is to tend to break up old conditions to make way for the new.

Neptune shows a total of (7) letters and a phonetic value of (29) or (2). These are Moon values, both the new and the full Moon symbols are shown. When we total these two numbers, (7) plus the (2) we get our human value (9). This is also an energy factor. Both the Moon and Neptune are associated with liquids and psychic phenomenon. In psychic phenomenon, the human instrument is involved, and, considerable personal energy is used. All individuals are cautioned about this factor when attending seances. This influence can be inspirational or fearful. Both of the Moon's values, positive and negative, make the total of (9). This is an energy value which can be used for good or ill. This particular planet is considered an enigma. It is considered the higher octave of Mercury, value (5), but, in this influence it is associated with psychic communication.

Pluto shows a total of (5) letters. This is also a mental factor and Pluto is associated with the subconscious mind. The phonetic values total to (27) or (9). This is our total number value and this planet is considered the higher octave of Mars, a

(9) value. This planet has considerable influence over group activities and its effects are so broad as to include all of humanity. When we add the (5) plus the (9) we total to (14), or (5). This planet's main influence, being a higher octave of Mars, is very subtle and is connected with subconscious communication and activity. When this energy factor of (9) is used constructively it can be used to seed the subconscious mind (5) which in turn can have broad effects upon the destiny and life of individuals.

In considering the astrological signs of our zodiac, we will start with Aries, the first house, or, angle of the wheel and proceed through the twelve in their regular numerical sequence.

Aries totals to (5) letters. The phonetic values total to (10) or (1). When we add these two factors (5) plus (1) we total to (6). This sign Aries is the exaltation angle of the Sun, indicated by the number (1). The (5) total letters also refers to the (5th) angle of the zodiac, which is ruled by the Sun. The (6) total value matches Venus, value (6), the planet of love. The fifth angle, amongst other things, rules love affairs. This sign Aries is also the detriment sign of Venus. All this information is conveyed in the cabalistic interpretation of this name, Aries.

Taurus totals to (6) letters. This sign is ruled by the planetary body, Venus, value (6). The phonetic value totals to (16) or (7). This is the Full Moon number (7) and this angle of our zodiac is the exaltation house of the Moon. The total letters (6) when added to the total phonetic value of (7) gives us a total of (13) or (4). This is the builder's symbol, also, it is the negative number of the Sun. Here there is a strong affinity for the love of money. Venus, value (6), planet of love, coupled with the full Moon number (7), symbol of fulfillment, adds to the negative number of the Sun, value (4). The second house or angle of our zodiac rules money and possessions.

Gemini totals to (6) letters and the phonetic values total to (15) or (6). The (6) plus (6) totals to our (3) value. Here the total letters and the total phonetic are both the symbol of Venus, the planet of love. Here the love manifests as love of relatives; brothers, sisters, aunts and uncles and etc. It also manifests as a love of knowledge, which falls under the rulership of the (3rd) angle of our zodiac. When these numbers are totaled we get our (3) value. When this knowledge is sifted and projected through the heart, wisdom results. Jupiter, value (3), rules the angle of higher learning and wisdom.

Cancer totals to (6) letters. The phonetic values total to (17) or (8). When we total the (6) plus the (8) we get (14) or (5). This sign cancer is the domestic sign, representative of the home and home environment. The (6) value is symbolical of Venus, planet of love, domestic love. The (8) is Saturn's number and denotes discipline. The total (5) is Mercury's number. The discipline in the domestic sphere, when administered through the process of love, benefits the children. The (5th) angle rules children, amongst other things. Also, (5) Mercury's symbol, is indicative of the mind. It is the intelligent discipline of the mind, or, mental process, through love, that we enjoy good health. Note that the mental organ, the brain, has (5) letters.

Right here we may note that the disease of cancer is perfectly diagnosed. Ease is the normal process of health. Dis-ease, denotes lack of ease, or, ill health. When cancer exists, the mental process needs disciplining through love. This condition of cancer is nothing more than deep-seated neurosis of hate or fear. Nothing manifests in the life of an individual unless it is in the mind first, conscious, or, subconscious. When we release the tensions, caused by the mental blocks, the life force of love, the divine breath, can heal the soul, and, in turn, the body.

Leo totals to (3) letters. The phonetic total adds to (10) or (1). When we total the (3) to the (1) we get our (4) value. Leo is the sign ruled by the Sun, values (1) and (4). It is natural that these numbers should show up in the totals of this name. The growth number (3) and the love number (6) are the only other numbers shown in the make-up of this name. Of course, we grow through love and the Sun generates this principle through the heart ruled by the Sun. This is another natural cabalistic name interpretation.

Virgo totals to (5) letters. The phonetic values total to (17) or (8). When we total the (5) plus the (8) we get our (13) or (4) value. The (5) is Mercury's number and Mercury rules this angle of the zodiac. The phonetic value (8) is Saturn's symbol, the number of discipline. The total value of (4) is the builder's symbol of the Sun. This house, or, angle of the zodiac governs health, work and service. When we discipline (8) our minds (5) we can build (4) soundly, either bodies, or, other structures. So, the (5), (8) and the (4) symbols are very indicative of the affairs and influences of this sign and name.

Libra totals to (5) letters and has a phonetic total value of (9). When we add the (5) plus the (9) we total to (14) or (5). This (5) is Mercury's number and it is considered neutral until aspected by another planet, or, is strong by sign. Libra has a similar influence in its symbolism. The scales are the symbol of this sign, and when empty they appear in perfect balance. Also, Libra is an air sign, as is Gemini, ruled by Mercury. This name Gemini also adds both in its letters and phonetic values to a (6) value, that of Venus which also rules Libra. We have noted that the (5th) angle of our zodiac rules the heart and love affairs. Libra tends to weigh decisions. The (9) value is the symbol of Mars. This planet is considered in its detriment in Libra. All action, symbolized by Mars, (9) value, is weighed in the balance and must give way to the (5th) angle influence of love. Libra love usually ends in partnerships or marriage, which also falls under the rulership of this sign.

Scorpio totals to (7) letters. This is the full Moon number. Scorpio is no milk and water influence. The full force of Mars is released through this sign as indicated by its phonetic value total, which nets to a (9) value. When we total the (7) plus the (9) we total to (16) or (7). This (7) symbolizes the total planetary values that activate our zodiacal wheel, and, Mars, value (9) which rules Scorpio, is considered the force or energy planet. Mars (9) coupled with the full Moon number (7) makes for much strength, force, magnetism and sex drive. This is the sex sign of the zodiac symbolized as regeneration.

Sagittarius totals to (11) or (2) letters. This is the new Moon number. The phonetic values total to (27) or (9). When we add the (2) plus the (9) we total to (11) or (2). This is a double bodied sign. Half human and half animal and is also symbolized by the arrow pointed upwards. Here the (2) value symbolizes the duality of humanity trying to conquer the lower animal nature as they strive for wisdom, the divine estate, symbolized by the (9) angle of the zodiac which this sign represents. This (9) is the human number indicative of the (9) orifices of the human or beast. The number (2) refers to this duality of the divine and the human. The new Moon value (2) also indicates that this is a new estate for which most of humanity is striving.

Capricorn totals to (9) letters. The phonetic value totals to (25) or (7). When we add the totals (9) plus the (7) we total to (16) or (7). In this total letters of (9) we have tremendous energy for achievement. The desire drive of the (9) value here is in the professional field, ruled by Capricorn. The phonetic and total value of the full Moon number (7) suggests the ability of full achievement. Complete full accomplishment in the professional field through the desire and force of the Mars value (9). Capricorn is the zenith of our zodiacal wheel and the (9) with the full Moon (7) indicates the total number (9) and the total planetary values (7) form a completeness for human achievement, which this angle, or, zodiacal house indicates.

Aquarius totals to (8) letters. The phonetic values total to (21) or (3). When we total the (8) plus the (3) we get (11) or (2). The total letters, (8) value, is the Saturn number which symbolizes age and limitation. The phonetic value (3) symbolizes growth through wisdom. The total value (2) is the new Moon number symbolizing a new beginning. Before the new age can begin the limitations of the past must be overcome through the growth in wisdom. By precession of the equinoxal movement in the zodiac, a new age is on the threshold, but, it must be achieved through wisdom as this name suggests.

Pisces totals to (6) letters. The phonetic values total to (22) or (4). When we add the (6) plus the (4) we total to (10) or (1). Pisces is a water sign in which the planet Venus, value (6) symbolized as love, is exalted. This sign of the fishes is ruled by Jupiter, value (3), the planet of growth. When we double Jupiter's symbol, the equilateral triangle, we have seen in a previous chapter how we create our (6) pointed star, symbolized by Venus, value (6). Pisces is the last sign of the zodiac symbolizing the end of a cycle. The phonetic value (4) is the builder's symbol and the (4th) angle of the chart in horary astrology denotes the end of the matter, of any question. The total of letters and phonetic, the (1) value, denotes the completed cycle. When the lesson of love, Venus value (6), has been learned and built, value (4), into the consciousness, then we have completed the circle, symbolized by this number (1).

As the readers can see, as they have progressed through this chapter of Astro-Numerical cabalistic interpretation, the English language cabala is good training for the development of the intuitive faculty. Much wisdom not found in books can be gained through its simple application.

Chapter 15
An Open Mind

With all the foregoing, I feel that this writing would not be complete without further comment on the virtue of keeping an open mind, before passing judgement on what has been written in this book.

The materialistic scientists through their particular way of thinking, feel fairly certain that life is a form of activity originating out of matter. That the combining of certain, as yet unknown, chemicals in a particular way will produce life. There is one obvious objection to such a theory, and, a most annoying one; Where did matter spring from?

It is foolish to think that some kind of primordial dust, existing in space, started to combine by some known, or, unknown law. When the physical scientists speak of matter at all, they are considering three-dimensional matter and its endless forms of activity.

Matter is made up of invisible atoms which are made up of a number of force fields, ad infinitum. So, there are endless dimensions in which so-called matter exists, the ultimate of which we can call mind. Now, if the scientists know nothing about any of the intermediate dimensions, except by possible mathematical deductions, they can have no conception whatsoever of the dimension called mind.

This ultimate called mind, nor any of the alleged dimensions existing between, are to be pictured as localized points in space, but, one and all are forms of activity.

When we consider the pro and con that has been raised on this particular subject by the greatest mentalities that the earth has ever known, often to the point of violence, without one bit of proof existing on either side, one can realize that the only persons satisfied with the answers were those who uttered them.

Much has been written on the evolution of humanity, but, humanity did not attain its present state by the laws of what our scientists, on this subject, call evolution. It is true that our physical body did. Form, or, shape is constantly undergoing the endless process of change. Change is the only true characteristic of so-called matter.

The false perceptions acquired by individuals in their efforts to arrive at some understandable relation between themselves and the world of matter in which they exist, have been brought about by faulty observation. Individuals have among their many other characteristics, a very dynamic force, called purpose. They must have this in everything that they do. Back of every act that we perform then lies this dynamic force of purpose. The purpose of any given act of an individual is not always apparent to another, and, it is not necessary that it should. The real reasons back of the acts are sometimes not even known consciously by the acting individual. But, subconsciously, we all do, and, in every detail. Not only do we know the purpose subconsciously, but, we also know what the results will be. Experiments with hypnosis have many times proven this fact.

In the world today we recognize two types of matter, namely, organic and inorganic. The organic is largely considered as animate. Yet, organic matter is constantly going through the process of becoming inorganic, and, vice versa. So, if this sort of interchange is going on between these two states of matter, they are not actually two different things, but, are one and the same. Organic means that which has organs, or, channels through which it carries on its particular functions. Physical humanity is made up of the same structural units as is all living form, and, that substance is called protoplasm with a nucleus. Some of these protoplasmic masses are extremely complicated. Some are simplified to such a low scale as to be without a nucleus. High or low, complicated or simple, they are all equally important to what is called life, on our physical plane.

All living things are in a process called growth. As for our classification of them by name such as, plant, animal, fish or fowl, it is for the sake of convenience. There are many plants that have characteristics of animals. There are many humans that display characteristics of animals. We should not be fooled by the human form into believing that we are necessarily seeing a human being. Yet, the nature of a thing, most usually, will be found in its actions, not its form.

We find that every civilization is a product of its time. All life works in perfectly harmonious rhythm, and, in that rhythm things are made manifest, or, caused to do what is called, come into being.

Right here it might be of interest to consider this word, rhythm, in the manner of our Astro-Numerical cabala. We find that the word rhythm has a total of (6) letters. This is the Venus value (6), symbolical of love. The phonetic values total to (16) or (7). When we total the (6) plus the (7) we get (13) or (4). The number (7) is the full Moon value of fruition, referring to completeness. The total (7) planetary values of our zodiac. The grand total (4) is the builder's symbol of the Sun, relating to the (4) triplicities of our zodiac, or, the (4) seasons of our earth. So, we can see that our whole system represents a rhythm, and, this rhythm is the love principle. When we multiply the total letters (6) by the total phonetic value (7) we total to (42) or (6). When we multiply this total (6) by the total number (4) we total to (24) or (6) again. So, this rhythm is definitely the love principle. Remember the expression —; God is love! This expression, God is love, totals to (9) letters. The phonetic values total to (18) or (9). This number when added to itself equals itself. This number (9) is the symbol of humanity. The motion of the Sun in the precession of the equinoxes, (72) years for (1) degree, totals to (7) plus (2) which gives us our (9). The cycle of our lunar body (27) days, adds (2) plus (7) to our total of (9). Of course the (9) orifices of the human species and the sum total of our numbers all fall into this rhythm.

This coming into, and, going out of being, takes place with the same kind of rhythmic perfection on all planes of consciousness, each according to its nature. This rhythm in occult phraseology is sometimes called, the Breath of Brahma. The Christian cabala referred to it as the Divine Breath, which we have noted in the previous chapter. Physiologists see it as the life and death cycle. But, whatever the terminology, when we come to understand this form of action, we will see how very beautiful it is, and, that life, of any kind, would be impossible without it.

In trying to keep an open mind, it is well to consider just how our mental process operates. We must remember that no two are alike, for each has its own particular rate of vibration. Yet, each must have a pole of diametrical opposition as well as one of attraction. It is in one or the other of these poles that mind force goes to work, manipulating matter, moulding it into three-dimensional form.

It is wrongly supposed that gravitational force is some form of three-dimensional energy at work. Gravitation is mind force working on, or, in chemical fields. It directs the electrons that spin around the atom, as well as the astronomical bodies that spin around the suns. Matter itself has neither shape or form other than that desired by mind, and, the seeming endlessness of matter is due to the fathomless nature of mind, which is without beginning or end. This is almost a definition of consciousness, or, the unknowable self.

At the present point of our civilization, we are still without the conscious knowledge of how to direct our thought forces to mold matter in visual form. It still remains as what we call a subconscious activity. This knowledge is still ours, but, it is buried deep within the subconscious. Some folks manifest this mind power through strong emotional desire such as faith healing and moving objects with a form of concentration, unknown to themselves that they are using this subconscious power, or, force. In our chapter on gambling we allude to this in a subtle manner.

It has been stated that neither humans or animals commit an act of any kind, good or bad, for the act itself. Nor because the act will bring pain or pleasure to another. Of course we can assume we know, but, our assumption would be based only upon our individual feeling as to what gives us pain or pleasure. Certain kinds of pleasure for one can be extreme pain to another, and, vice versa.

When one sets out to torture another, one does not start

doing so by conjuring up in the mind what mode of torture would be most unpleasant for that other, but, by imagining what would be most unbearable to oneself. A masochist is an inhibited sadist, and, a sadist is an inhibited masochist.

When giving alms to charity, one does so not because one is capable of sensing the great relief from lack it will bring to another, but, because the giving brings a bolstering of one's own ego and sense of self-security.

When a man and woman who claim to have great love for one another set out to culminate that love in the sex act, they seldom do so with the desire to bring pleasure to the other, but, strictly to themselves. In the few cases where they may really consider the other above themselves, their ideas are formed and acted upon by what brings the greatest sense of gratification to their own physical body and mind.

What we are trying to explain here is the fact that we are all unknown quantities to one another. One never comes face to face with another, but, what one comes face to face with oneself. Not knowing oneself, others appear as an X-quantity to the self. If we can accept all this to be true, it is not logical to obey the teaching of all the great teachers of humanity; that we love one another? For in so doing, we really love ourselves.

Subconscious and unconscious are practically the same states, for, all either of them can mean, is a different mode of awareness. Mind, being free, is not limited to any particular one of the endless modes of awareness. One can also hold a sense awareness to several modes at one and the same time. It is not advocated here that one should do so, because that state of duality is not for one's best interest. One can learn little, and, that little will be much too confusing to gain anything of worth. To really comprehend what is going on upon one plane, it is by far better to block off all the other. This is exactly what nature does. Natural sleep is nature's way of blocking off our outward state of consciousness. This gives rest to the physical body, and, brings into action the mental body. The various stages of trance are the blocking off of the different modes of consciousness so that the mental body can be entirely free on the one particular plane where the self is seeking to function.

Present day scientists are struggling with great difficulty trying to explain the extra-sensory functions of the mind. These functions and activities are called paranormal, simply because they are in such little use and therefore little understood. This subject has been dealt with in an exhaustive manner by some of the world's greatest scientific minds.

In space-time consciousness, we find a definite dimension of consciousness, such as we experience in physical consciousness. This we define as the mental plane. If space-time was an existing condition, separate from consciousness, then consciousness could never become aware of it. Space-time is consciousness and is everywhere present. It never began, and, shall therefore never end. There is no motion to it. That which we see in motion is a creation of it. Consciousness, and these endless states of motion are moulded into gases, liquids and solids, according to the needs of the varied and endless modes of consciousness. Some of these modes are what physical humanity calls time and environment.

Now, in respect to the physical brain of humanity, and, animals as well, there is a brain wave. These brain waves are the points of contact between the mode of consciousness called the physical humanity and another mode of consciousness called the spirit, or, higher self of each individual of the human race. It is by the strength of these brain waves that the higher self makes all of its so-called sense contacts with the physical world. They are created by the chemical composition of the body. If the body becomes chemically maladjusted, a small, or, large change takes place in these brain waves. The higher-self senses that change and the physical individual feels out of harmony with life, calling it sickness, blindness, deafness or lacking in one way or another. Harmony, or, ease is the health state. Lack of harmony, or, disease is the ill state.

These chemical mutations are constantly taking place in the body, but, no two bodies are affected in precisely the same manner. The self-consciousness of each individual interprets these changes in its own way. The effects, therefore, are not brought about so much by the actual chemical changes, as by what the self-consciousness of that particular body has learned to consider as being normal, or, abnormal to it.

This is why hypnosis is capable of bringing about a so-called cure, or, re-adjustment of the ill condition of the physical body, including the brain. The physical extension of the mind, called the body, is placed in abeyance by the trance state, and, the self is engaged in a calm and reasonable conversation. It is told that the chemical change that is giving it discomfort can be changed back to normal. The physical body, with its stresses of beliefs, being disassociated from the mind, then will not argue against the constructive suggestions. When the self again is given conscious control of its physical extension, it will go to work bringing about the necessary changes. The spoken words of the hypnotist become engraved in the consciousness of the higher-self in the form of stress lines. Becoming aware of its physical vehicle again, these stress lines will, in turn, be impressed upon the cells of the physical brain that operates the nervous system. The nervous system accepts the suggestions, and, imparts the message to the glandular system. This then excites the cells of the glands into manufacturing the proper chemicals which will then be carried by the blood stream and will rapidly bring back to normal the offending parts of the body.

Now the foregoing mechanistic approach does work, and, is much more effective than doctors and drugs. But, as we have noted in chapter twelve, the prayer as given in the Christian bible, is sufficient for all our ills, bodily, social or otherwise. The repetition of the Lord's Prayer, through the love principle in the heart, can also seed the subconscious with very much the same constructive effects in the life. All we have to do, is dare to believe, and, keep an open mind. As the folks say today, keep the faith!

In light of the foregoing, we should not close this writing without a very appropriate cabalistic interpretation of our words, open mind. Here we have two words with double unit force of (4) plus (4) which total to (8) letters. This is the builder's symbol of the Sun (4) which rules the (5th) angle of our zodiac, that of the heart and love. These values add to the (8) value of Saturn, the planetary value of discipline and karma. Karma, we have noted, is also of the love principle. The

(5) letters and the (1) phonetic value add to our (6) symbol of Venus, the planetary value of love. Here we build the love principle through discipline of the mind. The phonetic value of (open) totals to (20) or (2). The phonetic value of (mind) totals to (14) or (5). When we total these two values we get (2) plus (5) to a total of (7). Through these numbers we read that we have to accept new (2) ideas (5) to be able to achieve the fullness (7) of the mental benefits. The total of the (8) letters and the (7) phonetic add to a total of (15) or (6). Again we get our love principle. This (6) is also the number of Christ. This word has a total of (6) letters and the total phonetic adds to (15) or (6). This name is a double unit force of the love principle. When we add the (6) plus the (6) we total to (12) or (3). This is the number of our greater fortune of the zodiac, Jupiter, which is our value of growth and wisdom. We might also mention that Venus, the planet of love value (6) is exalted in the (12th) house or angle of our zodiac that of Pisces ruled by Jupiter value (3). This is the sign of the Fishes and Faith. The whole Christian era, for the last two thousand years, with the precession of the equinoxes tenanting this sign, has had tremendous influence on all of humanity. The symbolism of the Christ, the Faith and the Fishes all personify this love.

This is the lesson for all of humanity, the lesson of love, and the most necessary factor to achieve this is an open mind. For in keeping an open mind, we open our hearts to love.

Chapter 16
In Conclusion

The subject of astrology, as it is portrayed today, fails to impress a lot of folks because it has never been properly understood. In this book we have tried to give a better picture. One that can be interpreted in simple numbers and added up.

Basically, astrology is spiritual and mental as well as a physical science. This is one of the main objections that astronomers have against astrology. Not all astronomers, but most object to this spiritual and mental part of the science. Even the astrologers differ amongst themselves as to the rulerships of the astrological houses, or, angles of our zodiac. Some even throw up their hands in a state of shock when one even mentions the subject of numerology. Many religious sects advise their members to avoid these subjects. As for our English cabala, well, we are breaking new ground here.

This book was written in the manner that it was for a purpose. This purpose was to show that all life is one, interrelated process which stems from the invisible source.

As we have stated in chapter one, we are divine beings, and, as such, we are creators. It has been said; "Life is what you make it!" In this writing we have tried to show how it can be made more interesting. Through our cabala we find that the word, (life), reflects in its numerical values, the solar body. Here we have a (4) lettered word with a net phonetic value of (3). When we total these two values, the (4) plus the (3) we get (7). Our word Sun shows (3) for the letters and a net of (4) for the phonetic. These add (3) plus (4) to (7). As above, so below, is clearly reflected here in these two words. Our cycle around the Sun creates our four seasons, which, in turn, creates all our life on earth. Our Sun's numbers, the one and the four, also reflect these values in the written word.

The word (one), (3) letters plus a net of (4) for the phonetic totals to (7). The word (four), (4) letters plus a net of (3) for the phonetic totals to (7). These numbers reflect our growth, activity and fulfillment symbols.

There is one point that should be made clear. When one is analyzing words simply for definitive purposes, the words must always be considered in their generally accepted terms. For example, we can use the words blackmail and hijack. The word (blackmail) is a (9) lettered word with a net phonetic value of (7) which totals to a net of (7). This is a criminal act, so, we would say that this word shows the fullness (7) of power (9) in a criminal vein. The word (hijack) shows (6) letters and a net of (6) for the phonetic. When we add the (6) plus the (6) we total to a net of (3). This is also a criminal act. So, instead of interpreting it as a love (6) and wisdom (3) principle, we interpret it as a criminal act of money (6) and growth (3) effect, or, a criminal opportunity symbolized by the (3) to get something of value (6). Perhaps a little more word analysis would be of help to understand how so called mysteries may be less ambiguous. Watergate is a term that we have heard many times in recent years. Here we have a (9) lettered word with a net phonetic of (3). When we add the (9) plus the (3) we net to (12), or, (3). Of course the original act was a burglary, but, the term Watergate was used to identify the growth of political power abuse. Our number (9) for the total letters is our energy or force symbol. The (3) is our growth principle. So, this word's number values do reflect its popular accepted interpretation.

When we consider the word (death), we find that it has a total of (5) letters and a net of (5) for the phonetic. When we total the (5) plus the (5) we net to (10), or, (1). The (5) value is our transportation and communication symbol. Here it is concerned with a transition, or, passage from one state to another. The (1) value is our individual number, as well as indicating a beginning. It is also a number of completeness. Our numbers very aptly describe our interpretation of this word and act. It is interesting to note that the word (birth), is also a (5) lettered word with a net of (5) for the phonetic. These numbers, the (5) plus the (5) also total to a net of (10), or, (1). The same interpretation covers the birth act. So, through our astrological numerical cabala we find that death and birth are quite similar. Transition from the spiritual to the physical and from the physical to the spiritual is nothing more than the (1) life in its eternal motion.

Another word that we might relate here is (mystery). Here we have a (7) for the total letters and a net of (1) for the phonetic. These add (7) plus the (1) to our (8) value. The (7) is our full Moon number, indicating fullness of the lunar cycle. The (1) is also a number of completeness of the authoritative solar body. It is also our individualistic symbol. The (8) value is our symbol of eternity, as well as limitation. This word does convey limited understanding. Surely with our cabalistic word interpretations the only mystery that can be possible is the source of all being.

In our cabalistic process we have used (letters), (phonetic) and (net). This process fits our number and zodiacal rhythm. These words, (letters), (7) total letters, (phonetic), (8) total letters, and (net), (3) total letters add (7) plus (8) plus (3) to (18), or, (1) plus (8) to (9). The phonetic values total (8) plus (9) plus (1) to (18), or, (1) plus the (8) to (9).

Our numbers (1) through (9) add to a total of (45), or, (4) plus the (5) to (9).

When we consider the word (consciousness), which in the last analysis covers everything, we total to (13) letters, or, (1) plus the (3) to our (4). The phonetic totals to a net of (5). When we add the (4) plus the (5) we total to our (9).

The word (zodiac) totals to (6) for the letters. The phonetic nets to (3). When we add the (6) plus the (3) we total to (9). The zodiac is an inscribed circle in the heavens, actually our path around the solar orb. A circle is mathematically described as (360) degrees. When we add the (3) plus the (6) plus the (0) we total to our (9).

Our phrase, Man Know Thyself, adds (5) letters plus a phonetic of (4) which totals to (9).

Our solar body's motion in the precession of the equinoxes is (1) degree per (72) years. The (7) plus the (2) totals to our (9).

The lunar body transits the zodiac in (27) days. The (2) plus the (7) totals to (9).

In the human body, our heart, ruled by the Sun, beats at roughly (72) to the minute. The average span of life is approximately (72) years. Of course these add (7) plus the (2) to our (9) value. Also the human body has (9) orifices. Is it any wonder why number (9) is considered the human number?

All is related and all is one. All is rhythm. The word (all) has a total of (3) letters and a total of (4) for its phonetic value. When we total these values (3) plus (4) we get a total of (7). These are also the number factors for the (one).

Rhythm is a (6) lettered word with a phonetic total a net of (7). The (6) plus the (7) adds to (13), or, (1) plus (3) to (4). This (4) is the activity number of the Sun, as well as the builders symbol. When we write our numbers in their letters they match their total (9), as well as the builders number of the Sun.

(One), (3) letters, (4) phonetic to a net of (7).
(Two), (3) letters, (1) phonetic to a net of (4).
(Three), (5) letters, (3) phonetic to a net of (8).
(Four), (4) letters, (3) phonetic to a net of (7).
(Five), (4) letters, (6) phonetic to a net of (1).
(Six), (3) letters, (6) phonetic to a net of (9).
(Seven), (5) letters, (1) phonetic to a net of (6).
(Eight), (5) letters, (5) phonetic to a net of (1).
(Nine), (4) letters, (2) phonetic to a net of (6).

To recap the letters we show a total of (36), or, (3) plus the (6) to a total of (9). The phonetic values total to (31), or, (3) plus the (1) to (4). Those totals add (9) plus the (4) to (13), or, (1) plus the (3) to (4).

Our word, (related), as used in the past tense, shows a total of (7) letters. The phonetic also totals to a net of (7). When we add the (7) plus the (7) we get (14), or, (1) plus the (4) to (5). The (5) is our communication symbol, and, formed by the addition of the two (7)'s, shows that when we have related, we have communicated in full.

When we total the numerical value rulerships of the angles, or, houses of our zodiac wheel they also fit this cabalistic rhythm factor of (7) plus (6) to (13), or, (4).

Aries (9), Taurus (6), Gemini (5), Cancer (2 and 7) to (9), Leo (1 and 4) to (5), Virgo (5), Libra (6), Scorpio (9), Sagittarius (3),

Capricorn (8), Aquarius (8) and Pisces (3) add to (76), or, (7) plus the (6) to (13), or, (1) plus the (3) to a net of (4).

Continuing our additions of our houses or angles we can add (1) plus (2) plus (3) plus (4) plus (5) plus (6) plus (7) plus (8) plus (9) plus (10) plus (11) plus (12) to a total of (78) or (7) plus (8) to (15) or (1) plus (5) to a net of (6). Then if we add our houses to the net of the rulerships we show (6) plus (4) to a total of (10) or (1). This is our number of completeness (1), or, the net result of our Christening (6) activity (4).

In our cabalistic interpretations of the names of our planets and signs, in chapter (14), titled Cabala and Alchemy, we find that their net number values (total letters, total phonetic added to a net figure) totaled and added to the total number of planets and signs add to this Christening process.

For the planets we show; Sun (7), Moon (1), Mercury (8), Venus (7), Saturn (8), Jupiter (5), Mars (8), Uranus (2), Neptune (9) and Pluto (5) which total to (60) or (6). When we total the (10) (number of planets) to the total of the nets (6) we total to (16) or (7).

For the signs; Aries (6), Taurus (4), Gemini (3), Cancer (5), Leo (4), Virgo (4), Libra (5), Scorpio (7), Sagittarius (2), Capricorn (7), Aquarius (2) and Pisces (1) which total to (50) or (5). When we total the (12) (number of signs) to the total of the nets for the names (5) we add to (17) or (1) plus (7) to (8).

The total (7) for the planets and the total (8) for the signs add to (15) or (1) plus the (5) to our (6).

In reality, we are all caught up in the evolution of Christianity, which is our solar system, and we are all being Christened, whether we are aware of it or not. For (6) is the Venus number of Love and of Christ. Remember in the name, Christ, we have a (6) lettered word with a (6) phonetic which adds to a total of (12), our number of signs, and, also nets to a (3), our Jupiter symbol of growth which rules the ninth angle of our zodiac, that of Sagittarius which governs religion amongst other things. So ours is a divine rhythm, our numbers, planets and signs. An open book in the heavens for all to read and all we have to do is raise our heads and behold all the wonders of creation.

Taking the title of this book, Know Your Number, we total to a net of (14) or (1) plus the (4) to (5) for the letters. The phonetic also totals to (14) or (5). When we add the letters (5) to the phonetic (5) we total to (10) or (1). The (5) is our communication symbol and the (1) is our number of completeness. I trust that the readers will feel that in this book we have communicated in full.

The End.

On the following pages are the astrological planetary hours for 25 degrees through 55 degrees in north and south latitudes for January through December shown in their *numerical* planetary values.

Note:

This material is included here for easy reference for those readers who may be interested in selecting the most favorable periods for their social, business and recreational activities. These are to be used in conjunction with the values described in chapters (9) and (10).

Table of Planetary Hours
December and January in North Latitude
June and July in South Latitude
Hours Rulers and Days

Sun	Mon	Tues	Wed	Thurs	Fri	Sat	Degrees 25-35	35-45	45-55
			Sunrise				**A.M.**	**A.M.**	**A.M.**
1-4	2-7	9	5	3	6	8	6:58	7:25	8:05
6	8	1-4	2-7	9	5	3	7:48	8:10	8:45
5	3	6	8	1-4	2-7	9	8:38	8:56	9:24
2-7	9	5	3	6	8	1-4	9:29	9:42	10:03
8	1-4	2-7	9	5	3	6	10:19	10:28	10:42
3	6	8	1-4	2-7	9	5	11:10	11:14	11:21
			Noon				**P.M.**	**P.M.**	**P.M.**
9	5	3	6	8	1-4	2-7	0:00	0:00	0:00
1-4	2-7	9	5	3	6	8	0:50	0:46	0:39
6	8	1-4	2-7	9	5	3	1:41	1:32	1:18
5	3	6	8	1-4	2-7	9	2:31	2:18	1:57
2-7	9	5	3	6	8	1-4	3:22	3:04	2:36
8	1-4	2-7	9	5	3	6	4:12	3:50	3:15
			Sunset				**P.M.**	**P.M.**	**P.M.**
3	6	8	1-4	2-7	9	5	5:20	4:35	3:55
9	5	3	6	8	1-4	2-7	6:12	5:50	5:15
1-4	2-7	9	5	3	6	8	7:22	7:40	6:36
6	8	1-4	2-7	9	5	3	8:31	8:18	7:57
5	3	6	8	1-4	2-7	9	9:41	9:32	9:18
2-7	9	5	3	6	8	1-4	10:50	10:46	10:39
			Midnight				**A.M.**	**A.M.**	**A.M.**
8	1-4	2-7	9	5	3	6	0:00	0:00	0:00
3	6	8	1-4	2-7	9	5	1:10	1:14	1:21
9	5	3	6	8	1-4	2-7	2:19	2:28	2:42
1-4	2-7	9	5	3	6	8	3:29	3:42	4:30
6	8	1-4	2-7	9	5	3	4:38	4:56	5:24
5	3	6	8	1-4	2-7	9	5:48	6:10	6:45

Table of Planetary Hours
November and February in North Latitude
May and August in South Latitude
Hours Rulers and Days

| | | | | | | | Degrees | | |
Sun	Mon	Tues	Wed	Thurs	Fri	Sat	25-35	35-45	45-55
			Sunrise				**A.M.**	**A.M.**	**A.M.**
1-4	2-7	9	5	3	6	8	6:38	6:56	7:20
6	8	1-4	2-7	9	5	3	7:31	7:46	8:07
5	3	6	8	1-4	2-7	9	8:25	8:37	8:54
2-7	9	5	3	6	8	1-4	9:19	9:28	9:40
8	1-4	2-7	9	5	3	6	10:12	10:18	10:27
3	6	8	1-4	2-7	9	5	11:07	11:09	11:13
			Noon				**P.M.**	**P.M.**	**P.M.**
9	5	3	6	8	1-4	2-7	0:00	0:00	0:00
1-4	2-7	9	5	3	6	8	0:54	0:51	0:47
6	8	1-4	2-7	9	5	3	1:48	1:42	1:34
5	3	6	8	1-4	2-7	9	2:42	2:32	2:20
2-7	9	5	3	6	8	1-4	3:35	3:23	3:06
8	1-4	2-7	9	5	3	6	4:29	4:14	3:53
			Sunset				**P.M.**	**P.M.**	**P.M.**
3	6	8	1-4	2-7	9	5	5:22	5:04	4:40
9	5	3	6	8	1-4	2-7	6:29	6:14	5:53
1-4	2-7	9	5	3	6	8	7:35	7:23	7:06
6	8	1-4	2-7	9	5	3	8:42	8:32	8:20
5	3	6	8	1-4	2-7	9	9:48	9:42	9:34
2-7	9	5	3	6	8	1-4	10:54	10:51	10:47
			Midnight				**A.M.**	**A.M.**	**A.M.**
8	1 4	2 7	9	5	3	6	0:00	0:00	0:00
3	6	8	1-4	2-7	9	5	1:06	1:09	1:13
9	5	3	6	8	1-4	2-7	2:12	2:18	2:27
1-4	2-7	9	5	3	6	8	3:19	3:28	3:40
6	8	1-4	2-7	9	5	3	4:25	4:37	4:54
5	3	6	8	1-4	2-7	9	5:31	5:46	6:07

Table of Planetary Hours
October and March in North Latitude
April and September in South Latitude
Hours Rulers and Days

Sun	Mon	Tues	Wed	Thurs	Fri	Sat		25-35	35-45	45-55
			Sunrise					A.M.	A.M.	A.M.
1-4	2-7	9	5	3	6	8		6:19	6:27	6:39
6	8	1-4	2-7	9	5	3		7:15	7:22	7:32
5	3	6	8	1-4	2-7	9		8:12	8:18	8:26
2-7	9	5	3	6	8	1-4		9:09	9:13	9:19
8	1-4	2-7	9	5	3	6		10:06	10:09	10:13
3	6	8	1-4	2-7	9	5		11:03	11:04	11:06
			Noon					P.M.	P.M.	P.M.
9	5	3	6	8	1-4	2-7		0:00	0:00	0:00
1-4	2-7	9	5	3	6	8		0:57	0:56	0:54
6	8	1-4	2-7	9	5	3		1:54	1:51	1:47
5	3	6	8	1-4	2-7	9		2:51	2:47	2:41
2-7	9	5	3	6	8	1-4		3:48	3:42	3:34
8	1-4	2-7	9	5	3	6		4:45	4:38	4:28
			Sunset					P.M.	P.M.	P.M.
3	6	8	1-4	2-7	9	5		5:41	5:33	5:21
9	5	3	6	8	1-4	2-7		6:45	6:38	6:28
1-4	2-7	9	5	3	6	8		7:48	7:42	7:34
6	8	1-4	2-7	9	5	3		8:51	8:47	8:41
5	3	6	8	1-4	2-7	9		9:54	9:51	9:47
2-7	9	5	3	6	8	1-4		10:57	10:56	10:54
			Midnight					A.M.	A.M.	A.M.
8	1-4	2-7	9	5	3	6		0:00	0:00	0:00
3	6	8	1-4	2-7	9	5		1:03	1:04	1:06
9	5	3	6	8	1-4	2-7		2:06	2:09	2:13
1-4	2-7	9	5	3	6	8		3:09	3:13	3:19
6	8	1-4	2-7	9	5	3		4:12	4:18	4:26
5	3	6	8	1-4	2-7	9		5:15	5:22	5:32

Table of Planetary Hours
April and September in North Latitude
October and March in South Latitude
Hours Rulers and Days

| | | | | | | | Degrees | | |
Sun	Mon	Tues	Wed	Thurs	Fri	Sat	25-35	35-45	45-55
			Sunrise				**A.M.**	**A.M.**	**A.M.**
1-4	2-7	9	5	3	6	8	5:41	5:33	5:21
6	8	1-4	2-7	9	5	3	6:45	6:38	6:28
5	3	6	8	1-4	2-7	9	7:48	7:42	7:34
2-7	9	5	3	6	8	1-4	8:51	8:47	8:41
8	1-4	2-7	9	5	3	6	9:54	9:51	9:47
3	6	8	1-4	2-7	9	5	10:57	10:56	10:54
			Noon				**P.M.**	**P.M.**	**P.M.**
9	5	3	6	8	1-4	2-7	0:00	0:00	0:00
1-4	2-7	9	5	3	6	8	1:03	1:04	1:06
6	8	1-4	2-7	9	5	3	2:06	2:09	2:13
5	3	6	8	1-4	2-7	9	3:09	3:13	3:19
2-7	9	5	3	6	8	1-4	4:12	4:18	4:26
8	1-4	2-7	9	5	3	6	5:15	5:22	5:32
			Sunset				**P.M.**	**P.M.**	**P.M.**
3	6	8	1-4	2-7	9	5	6:19	6:27	6:39
9	5	3	6	8	1-4	2-7	7:15	7:22	7:32
1-4	2-7	9	5	3	6	8	8:12	8:18	8:26
6	8	1-4	2-7	9	5	3	9:09	9:13	9:19
5	3	6	8	1-4	2-7	9	10:06	10:09	10:13
2-7	9	5	3	6	8	1-4	11:03	11:04	11:06
			Midnight				**A.M.**	**A.M.**	**A.M.**
8	1-4	2-7	9	5	3	6	0:00	0:00	0:00
3	6	8	1-4	2-7	9	5	0:57	0:56	0:54
9	5	3	6	8	1-4	2-7	1:54	1:51	1:47
1-4	2-7	9	5	3	6	8	2:51	2:47	2:41
6	8	1-4	2-7	9	5	3	3:48	3:42	3:34
5	3	6	8	1-4	2-7	9	4:45	4:38	4:28

Table of Planetary Hours
May and August in North Latitude
November and February in South Latitude
Hours Rulers and Days

| | | | | | | | Degrees | | |
Sun	Mon	Tues	Wed	Thurs	Fri	Sat	25-35	35-45	45-55
			Sunrise				A.M.	A.M.	A.M.
1-4	2-7	9	5	3	6	8	5:22	5:04	4:40
6	8	1-4	2-7	9	5	3	6:29	6:14	5:53
5	3	6	8	1-4	2-7	9	7:35	7:23	7:06
2-7	9	5	3	6	8	1-4	8:42	8:32	8:20
8	1-4	2-7	9	5	3	6	9:48	9:42	9:34
3	6	8	1-4	2-7	9	5	10:54	10:51	10:47
			Noon				P.M.	P.M.	P.M.
9	5	3	6	8	1-4	2-7	0:00	0:00	0:00
1-4	2-7	9	5	3	6	8	1:06	1:09	1:13
6	8	1-4	2-7	9	5	3	2:12	2:18	2:27
5	3	6	8	1-4	2-7	9	3:19	3:28	3:40
2-7	9	5	3	6	8	1-4	4:25	4:37	4:54
8	1-4	2-7	9	5	3	6	5:31	5:46	6:07
			Sunset				P.M.	P.M.	P.M.
3	6	8	1-4	2-7	9	5	6:38	6:56	7:20
9	5	3	6	8	1-4	2-7	7:31	7:46	8:07
1-4	2-7	9	5	3	6	8	8:25	8:37	8:54
6	8	1-4	2-7	9	5	3	9:19	9:28	9:40
5	3	6	8	1-4	2-7	9	10:12	10:18	10:27
2-7	9	5	3	6	8	1-4	11:07	11:09	11:13
			Midnight				A.M.	A.M.	A.M.
8	1-4	2-7	9	5	3	6	0:00	0:00	0:00
3	6	8	1-4	2-7	9	5	0:54	0:51	0:47
9	5	3	6	8	1-4	2-7	1:48	1:42	1:34
1-4	2-7	9	5	3	6	8	2:42	2:32	2:20
6	8	1-4	2-7	9	5	3	3:35	3:23	3:06
5	3	6	8	1-4	2-7	9	4:29	4:14	3:53

Table of Planetary Hours
June and July in North Latitude
December and January in South Latitude
Hours Rulers and Days

Sun	Mon	Tues	Wed	Thurs	Fri	Sat	Degrees 25-35	35-45	45-55
			Sunrise				A.M.	A.M.	A.M.
1-4	2-7	9	5	3	6	8	5:02	4:35	3:55
6	8	1-4	2-7	9	5	3	6:12	5:50	5:15
5	3	6	8	1-4	2-7	9	7:22	7:04	6:36
2-7	9	5	3	6	8	1-4	8:31	8:18	7:57
8	1-4	2-7	9	5	3	6	9:41	9:32	9:18
3	6	8	1-4	2-7	9	5	10:50	10:46	10:39
			Noon				P.M.	P.M.	P.M.
9	5	3	6	8	1-4	2-7	0:00	0:00	0:00
1-4	2-7	9	5	3	6	8	1:10	1:14	1:21
6	8	1-4	2-7	9	5	3	2:19	2:28	2:42
5	3	6	8	1-4	2-7	9	3:29	3:42	4:03
2-7	9	5	3	6	8	1-4	4:38	4:56	5:24
8	1-4	2-7	9	5	3	6	5:48	6:10	6:45
			Sunset				P.M.	P.M.	P.M.
3	6	8	1-4	2-7	9	5	6:58	7:25	8:05
9	5	3	6	8	1-4	2-7	7:48	8:10	8:45
1-4	2-7	9	5	3	6	8	8:38	8:56	9:24
6	8	1-4	2-7	9	5	3	9:29	9:42	10:03
5	3	6	8	1-4	2-7	9	10:19	10:28	10:42
2-7	9	5	3	6	8	1-4	11:10	11:14	11:21
			Midnight				A.M.	A.M.	A.M.
8	1-4	2-7	9	5	3	6	0:00	0:00	0:00
3	6	8	1-4	2-7	9	5	0:50	0:46	0:39
9	5	3	6	8	1-4	2-7	1:41	1:32	1:18
1-4	2-7	9	5	3	6	8	2:31	2:18	1:57
6	8	1-4	2-7	9	5	3	3:22	3:04	2:36
5	3	6	8	1-4	2-7	9	4:12	3:50	3:15